"John Strege is a captivating stor, latest and most important work. In *A Snowflake Named Hannah*, John pulls back the curtain on the seemingly mysterious world of embryo adoption and candidly shares the miraculous, pioneering journey that has changed the course of human history."

PAUL J. BATURA, vice president of communications for
Focus on the Family

"John, Marlene, and Hannah Strege are integral to the creation and history of embryo adoption. Now families have welcomed over seven hundred babies who otherwise would still be frozen in liquid nitrogen in a fertility clinic. John and Marlene are tireless promoters, connectors, speakers, and leaders for this unique form of adoption, and it all started with *A Snowflake Named Hannah*, the story of Snowflake baby number one."

KIMBERLY TYSON, executive director of the Snowflakes Embryo
Adoption Program

"John Strege is a friend and a talented author. Thanks to Marlene and John stepping out in faith, a beautiful girl is now living a wonderful life. Open the pages of this gripping book and read their remarkable story."

JIM DALY, president of Focus on the Family

"One of the unlikeliest and most impactful books I have ever read. John is a gifted sportswriter and, it turns out, a tribune of life with the pen. This book, like Hannah herself, makes a powerful case against embryonic stem cell research and for embryo adoption. All you can do is marvel at the life and testimony of Hannah, Marlene, and John—and pass along this amazing book, which may bring forth many other precious lives and will inspire a renewed focus on the central truth at the heart of these debates: life is a precious gift and needs our collective protection from conception until the last breath."

HUGH HEWITT, host of the nationally syndicated *Hugh Hewitt Show*

"John Strege provides a powerful narrative of the history of embryo adoption from a father's perspective. The attention to detail and obvious love John has for God and his family make the pages come to life. Hannah's story speaks to the importance of every child and all forms of adoption."

CHRISTINA SUZANN NELSON, author of *Swimming in the Deep End*

"Nothing could be more life-affirming than the miracle that Hannah is. Need evidence and inspiration that God is the author of life? Read Hannah's story."

CHRIS MORTENSEN, senior reporter at ESPN

A Snowflake Named Hannah

A Snowflake Named Hannah

Ethics, Faith, and the First Adoption
of a Frozen Embryo

JOHN STREGE

KREGEL
PUBLICATIONS

To Ron Stoddart, Dr. James Dobson,
the late Rev. Dr. Charles Manske,
and Rev. Robert Dargatz

And to Marlene,
who conceived of the
inconceivable

Before I formed you in the womb I knew you,
before you were born I set you apart.

JEREMIAH 1:5

For we walk by faith, not by sight.

2 CORINTHIANS 5:7 (NKJV)

Contents

Foreword
by Hannah Strege

MY ADOPTION STORY was never a secret to me. I was the first adopted frozen embryo and was made aware of it at a very early age. I knew that I was one of twenty frozen embryos adopted from my placing family and that my mom is both my birth mom and·my adoptive mom, though I did not necessarily understand what that meant initially.

Explaining embryo adoption to an adult, let alone a young child, isn't easy. My mom, being the creative individual she is, used kid-appropriate analogies with me. For instance, she took two packets of seeds—carrot and pumpkin—and put them in the freezer. We took them out of the freezer during the correct planting season. She and I carefully counted out twenty seeds from the packet, representing the twenty embryos that my parents had adopted. We then planted them in an egg carton to grow. Not all the seeds sprouted, just like not all the embryos survived the thaw. We eventually transferred the remaining seedlings into the garden, and not all the plants survived. Again, this represented how not all the embryos survived once they were transferred into my mom.

My mom explained that this was how she and my dad adopted my nineteen siblings and me as frozen seeds. She also said there was no guarantee that all twenty of the embryos would survive the freeze, the thaw, and the transfer. She said, "You were adopted as a seed and put into my tummy to grow."

As a young girl, that's how I attempted to explain my adoption story to others, though it may have been confusing and frustrating at times. I was surprised how often my friends and even adults did not know what

an embryo is. I also often received odd questions about my story. Here
are a few of my answers:

—Yes, I know who my "real parents" are. They're John and Marlene
    Strege. If you're referring to my placing family, yes, I know them
    too.
—No, my mom was not a surrogate.
—No, this was not a donor program.
—No, my parents did not adopt sperm.
—No, my parents did not adopt eggs.
—There is no possible way I share any DNA with my adoptive family.
—Open adoption is a way to know your child's genetic history. We
    enjoy an open adoption with my placing family, with no need for
    ancestry.com.
—No, I do not feel different being the first adopted frozen embryo.
    This is my life; it's all I know.

When we went to see the film *Heaven Is for Real*, the young boy,
Colton, was explaining to his mother his experience in heaven and
described the encounter he had with a young girl he said was his sister.
His mother was confused and noted that his sister, Cassie, was seated
behind him at the dining room table. No, Colton said. He had two sisters. "You had a baby die in your tummy, didn't you?"

His mother, stunned, asked who told him about that. Colton replied
that the girl herself had told him. His mother asked what the girl looked
like. "Like Cassie but a little smaller and hair like yours. In heaven
this little girl came up to me and she wouldn't stop hugging me." His
mother asked him what her name was. "She didn't have a name," Colton
replied. "You guys didn't name her." His mother had had a miscarriage.

The moment was a tearjerker and immediately caused us to turn our
hearts and minds to my nineteen siblings, the frozen embryos that did
not survive the freeze, the thaw, and the transfer. I decided we should

name them, and we did so as a family. The rule was that we all had to agree on the names. Their names:

Summer, Toby, Ryan, Delaney, Logan, Emma, Annika, Katiyana, Katelyn, McKenna, Gabe, Peyton, Spencer, Samuel, Megan, Leah, Levi, Hope, and Liesl.

This task wasn't as easy as one would think. Then I suggested we should give them middle names too. Isn't that an exhausting thought!

It was not until my teenage years that I became more curious about my placing family, though my love for my parents remained unwavering. I had a family, I was safe, and I had gotten a chance at life that many other frozen embryos had not. Still, I was eager to learn more about my placing family, maybe the only "normal" aspect of my otherwise unusual adoption. During my senior year of high school, I had the opportunity to do my senior project on the meaning of family. I concluded that one family holds my biology, and the other holds my heart.

I had a beloved teacher in high school ask me whether I had survivor's guilt as the only one of the twenty embryos to survive. I replied that I never felt that way because I knew the outcome was God's plan. But it has made me appreciate my chance at life, that it is that much more special. I even plan on devoting my career to the cause of life, specifically adoption as a means of countering abortion, and I related this in the following letter I wrote early in my freshman year of college to Vice President Mike Pence:

October 14, 2017
Dear Vice President Pence,

My name is Hannah Strege. When I was about seven years old, you and I met at a press conference in 2006 to highlight Snowflake babies. I had something to tell lawmakers and the President that day: "Don't kill the Snowflakes . . . we're kids and we want to grow up."

I am the first adopted frozen embryo in the world. My parents, John and Marlene Strege, adopted me and 19 other frozen embryos from a placing family through a program later named Snowflakes Embryo Adoption through Nightlight Christian Adoptions. Snowflakes are unique and never again to be re-created, just like each baby is molded in the likeness of God. My mom, Marlene, is both the adoptive mom and the birth mom.

I stood behind President George W. Bush during his first veto, in 2006, with regards to limiting federal funding for embryonic stem cell research. President Obama lifted the veto during his presidency. I know you and President Trump are pro-life and I am hoping you would consider stopping federal funding on embryonic stem cell research. I would ask that you share my story with President Trump. I would be happy to speak with anyone regarding embryo adoption. I am now a freshman in college at Biola University studying nursing. Saving embryos is a cause dear to my heart. Each frozen embryo is a life and we should be striving for plans of adoption instead of destruction.

For the embryos yet to be born,
Hannah Strege

Several weeks later, I received this letter from Vice President Pence:

Ms. Hannah Strege
La Mirada, California

Dear Hannah:

Thank you for your recent heartfelt letter. It was an honor to meet you years ago, and I am grateful that you reached out to me with an update.

Congratulations on your high school graduation and your

next step of college. Your determination not only to achieve academic success but also to stand for the dignity of the unborn is deeply inspiring. Your story of embryo adoption continues to move my heart. I am grateful for the privilege to serve a President who is committed to the cause of life. Please be assured that President Trump and I will continue to uphold the sanctity of human life and seek to restore pro-life principles to the center of American law.

Thank you for being a voice for the cause of life. You have my best wishes as you continue your nursing studies at Biola.

Sincerely,
Michael R. Pence
Vice President of the United States

I have since changed my major and am pursuing a bachelor's degree in sociology. My goal is to work toward a master's degree in social work. With these degrees I hope to help induce social change on abortion, the overuse of in vitro fertilization, and the creation of more embryos than a couple will be able to use—and to help rescue the embryos still in frozen storage. I want to give a voice to the voiceless. I owe it to my nineteen siblings. Their lives will not be forgotten.

Acknowledgments

THIS IS THE seventh book I've written, and simultaneously it was the hardest and easiest book for me to write. It was the easiest because we had lived it, and Marlene had kept meticulous notes as well as letters, emails, and newspaper and magazine articles. It was the hardest because it is so personal. For a sports journalist with an aversion to using the pronoun *I*, who is far more comfortable reporting the news than being a part of it, this was an awkward transition.

Easing the transition was the encouragement I received from so many over the years. I am especially indebted to Carl Catlin for his friendship and his Christian leadership in our church, and for his unceasing support for this project and others I've undertaken. Everyone should be so fortunate as to have a Carl Catlin in their lives.

Pastors Chuck Manske and Bob Dargatz have been an enormous blessing in our lives through their spiritual guidance and friendship. Everyone should be so fortunate as to have pastors such as these in their lives.

Ron Stoddart is an amazing individual whose love for children and passion for placing children with their forever families is an inspiration to all of us. There would be no story to tell had Ron viewed our request to adopt embryos as a time-consuming challenge rather than an opportunity to save lives. I spent the better part of two hours with Ron in a Loveland, Colorado, restaurant to get his recollections of the events recounted in these pages, and I thank him for that. Everyone should be so fortunate as to have a Ron Stoddart in their corner.

Fifty years in sports journalism dealing with professional athletes and other celebrities has nearly rid me of any sense of awe, yet I confess I stand in awe of Dr. James Dobson for his tireless devotion to family and Christian values and for his dogged defense of the sanctity of human life. What he has meant to our family and the cause of embryo adoption is incalculable, and we are eternally grateful. We are blessed to call him a friend.

JoAnn (Davidson) Eiman, affectionately known as J. D., was an integral part of our embryo adoption story and was indefatigable in committing her time and talents in getting the Snowflakes Embryo Adoption Program started. I tapped into her memory bank for her recollections of that time in our lives. A simple thank-you seems inadequate for the work she did on our behalf and for so many Snowflake babies that followed.

We are so grateful to all those at Focus on the Family, past and present, who were involved in our story and supported and embraced embryo adoption. These include Sydna Massé and Carrie Gordon Earll. Sydna was the point person in connecting us with the family that chose us to adopt their frozen embryos, and she happily recounted for me her memories of those days. Carrie, the vice president of government and public policy at Focus on the Family, eagerly embraced our cause and was instrumental in organizing our Washington, DC, trips.

Paul Batura, vice president of communications at Focus on the Family, his wife, Julie, and their three adopted children have become dear friends. Paul is a gifted writer whose latest book, *Chosen for Greatness: How Adoption Changes the World*, has been an inspiration and a source of encouragement to me. It should be as well to anyone considering adoption. Thank you, Paul.

Our church family at Zion Lutheran in Fallbrook, California, has continuously and enthusiastically supported us and our efforts to promote embryo adoption and tell Hannah's story. Thanks especially to our pastor, Rev. Aaron Pingel, and his wife, Kara, for their support.

I am grateful for those from the Snowflakes Embryo Adoption Program who shared their stories with me—Debbie Struiksma, Doni Brinkman, Courtney Atnip, Suzanne Murray, Heather Hutchens, Elizabeth Wilson, Lucinda McKenzie, Pastor Luke and Joni Timm, and Ruth Lawson. These are among the legion of Christians who selflessly advanced the cause and helped turn it into an important pro-life movement at a time when science was in need of a moral regulator.

Enough cannot be said for the staff at Nightlight Christian Adoptions, including Daniel Nehrbass, who had a tough act to follow when he was hired to succeed Ron Stoddart and has done so impressively, and Kimberly Tyson, the director of the Snowflakes Embryo Adoption Program, who has expertly guided and grown it. Both were interviewed for this project, and I thank them for their input.

Dana Chisholm, a passionate pro-life Christian, befriended Marlene at the outset of our story and fully embraced what we were trying to do. She also assisted me in finding an agent to represent this project. I thank her and that agent, Nick Harrison of WordServe Literary Group, who believed in this project and agreed to take it on.

The team at Kregel Publications—notably Steve Barclift, Katherine Chappell, Janyre Tromp, and Sarah De Mey—is an impressive one. Professional. Enthusiastic. Supportive. Helpful. It has been a pleasure working with everyone there.

Last but not least are the two most important people in this story, also the two most important in my life: Marlene and Hannah. Each has been a blessing to me, but together they've enriched my life beyond anything I could have imagined.

Introduction

THE EAST ROOM of the White House often has been the scene of somber occasions. This was not one of them. Early in the afternoon on July 19, 2006, twenty-four young children—many of them "little wigglers," as President George W. Bush called them—were on the East Room riser or in the audience with their parents, who had been invited there to bear witness to a historic stand on behalf of the sanctity of human life. The mood was celebratory.

My wife, Marlene, and our daughter, Hannah, adopted as a frozen embryo eight years earlier, took their assigned seats on the riser, just to the left of the presidential podium. Hannah was holding her small stuffed dog, named Lollipup, and was fidgety, as seven-year-olds are wont to be in formal settings. She was eager to return to the hotel swimming pool, though the baby on the lap of the woman next to her helped keep her somewhat occupied.

Finally, President Bush entered the room and strode to the podium to announce the first veto of his presidency, in his sixth year in office. It involved a bill Congress had passed, H.R. 810, that would have allowed federal funding for embryonic stem cell research that destroys human embryos in the process.

"This bill," President Bush said, "would support the taking of innocent human life in the hope of finding medical benefits for others. It crosses a moral boundary that our decent society needs to respect, so I vetoed it."

Those in the room erupted in applause. President Bush continued.

Like all Americans, I believe our nation must vigorously pursue the tremendous possibility that science offers to cure disease and improve the lives of millions. . . . Some scientists believe that one source of these cures might be embryonic stem cell research. Embryonic stem cells have the ability to grow into specialized adult tissues, and this may give them the potential to replace damaged or defective cells or body parts and treat a variety of diseases.

Yet we must also remember that embryonic stem cells come from human embryos that are destroyed for their cells. Each of these human embryos is a unique human life with inherent dignity and matchless value. We see that value in the children who are with us today. Each of these children began his or her life as a frozen embryo that was created for in vitro fertilization, but remained unused after the fertility treatments were complete. Each of these children was adopted while still an embryo, and has been blessed with the chance to grow up in a loving family.

These boys and girls are not spare parts.[1]

There it was: the most powerful man on earth speaking for those who cannot speak for themselves and distilling a complex issue into a simple truth: *These boys and girls are not spare parts.*

It was a momentous statement, and one that personally was the capstone of our journey that had begun nine years earlier with a simple desire to have a baby. God answered our prayers, but he did so in a way we never could have envisioned. Our adoption of frozen embryos evolved into a cause greater than ourselves by igniting a pro-life movement of a different sort, and a necessary one as science began to outrace ethical considerations.

Less than two months before Hannah was born, the world learned that stem cells extracted from human embryos could *potentially* lead to cures for a vast number of diseases, though the embryos would be destroyed in the process. Hannah's birth was a timely reminder of what was at stake here. She put a human face to the debate, as did those babies that followed via embryo adoption. This was never our intention, though it became a necessary step to help counter the push for research that crossed ethical and moral boundaries.

Was this God's plan? As events unfolded, we began to suspect we were not in control. There were too many coincidences, too many pieces to a difficult puzzle that had to fall into place just for us to have a baby, at precisely the same time help was required to buttress the pro-life side of a contentious controversy that would sweep President George W. Bush and Pope John Paul II into its purview.

"God calls everybody to use the gifts and the passion that they have," renowned pastor Rick Warren once wrote, "but not everyone picks up the phone."[2]

Marlene did answer the call, unaware where it might lead or even that it was leading anywhere. She faithfully followed the cues, and they led to the birth of Hannah and the creation of the Snowflakes Embryo Adoption Program at Nightlight Christian Adoptions in Orange County, California.

These then led us to Colorado Springs, Colorado, for a meeting with Dr. James Dobson at Focus on the Family. That meeting led us to his radio studio for the first of several radio broadcasts and resulted in an enduring friendship. Dr. Dobson, with his vast global influence, became a vitally important voice in introducing the world at large to embryo adoption, which in turn became the viable and visible alternative to the destruction of human embryos for research purposes and the proverbial slippery slope to cloning.

When embryonic stem cell research and its potential as a cure-all reached the mainstream and became a contentious political issue, it took us to Washington, DC, and the halls of Congress. In a congressional subcommittee hearing, Marlene and others argued against taxpayers funding the research that destroys the embryos, while facing formidable opposition that included Christopher Reeve, Michael J. Fox, and Mary Tyler Moore—each of whom we sympathized with and deeply admired.

We have this phrase displayed in our home: "God doesn't call the qualified. He qualifies the called." This was Marlene, who immersed herself in understanding the issues and became an eloquent and passionate advocate on behalf of those frozen embryos yet to be born. She studied up on the promising alternatives to using embryonic stem cells in research, including the use of adult and umbilical cord stem cells, which does not destroy human life.

Inevitably, her advocacy and passion to do what God has commanded, to care for the least of these, led our family and other Snowflake families to the White House on two occasions, in 2005 and 2006. We remain grateful to have had a staunchly pro-life president in office at the time. His veto did not stop embryonic stem cell research, but without federal funding, it did slow down substantially, buying time that allowed research on stem cells that does not destroy embryos to accelerate.

We have in a prominent place in our home a framed leaf from the first press run of the King James Bible from the year 1611. When I acquired it as an anniversary gift, I chose the leaf on which the book of Jeremiah begins, for the verse Jeremiah 1:5: "Before I formed thee in the belly I knew thee; and before thou camest forth out of the womb I sanctified thee, and I ordained thee a prophet unto the nations."

Jeremiah 1:5 has become our family verse. We have cited it frequently over the years in helping Hannah understand her roots and to explain the embryo adoption cause that she has enthusiastically embraced as morally and ethically the only alternative to research that destroys embryos.

Though the cause began with Hannah, it became a movement when many other Christian couples—most, but not all, with infertility issues—also embraced the idea of embryo adoption. Thousands of frozen embryos have thus been given a chance at life, not just through Nightlight Christian Adoptions but also through other adoption agencies and clinics around the country. In the years ahead, tens of thousands more frozen embryos are certain to be provided the same opportunity.

This is Hannah's story and our story, but it is theirs as well.

CHAPTER 1

What Would God Think?

LIFE GENERALLY HAD been good to Marlene and me in the eleven-plus years we had been married. We were both gainfully employed, Marlene as an occupational therapist and I as a sportswriter. We lived in a nice tract home in San Diego County. It had three bedrooms, two pets (a sheltie named Chelsea and a canary named Gordie), and one void.

We had no children.

We had put off having children for several years. Marlene had not had an opportunity to attend college following high school graduation, except for a brief stint at a community college. Together we made it a priority that she would pursue a degree and a career, so that if something happened to me, she still could comfortably support herself and our kids—once we had them. In 1991, she received her bachelor of science degree in occupational therapy from the University of Southern California and graduated magna cum laude.

Former Major League Baseball commissioner Peter Ueberroth was the USC commencement speaker that year, which interested me as a former baseball writer. Not long after witnessing Ueberroth's excellent commencement address, I needed to speak with him for a story I was working on for the *Orange County Register*. When I reached him by phone, I explained that I'd been there to hear his speech because my wife had graduated that day.

"Oh, what was her major?" Ueberroth asked.

"Occupational therapy," I said.

"She must be a caring person," he replied.

His observation was spot-on. Her first job was with Rancho Los Amigos National Rehabilitation Center in Downey, California. After our move to San Diego County she wound up at Sharp Hospital in San Diego, working in adult acute rehabilitation, often with patients who had suffered spinal cord injuries. In recent years, she has been employed by our local elementary school district, working with special needs kids.

We had our house in order, yet our house, five years after her graduation, still had two of its three bedrooms sadly unoccupied. Our next step was to find out why. We eventually went through costly, and unsuccessful, infertility treatments. We still retained hope that they might work, but our optimism was fading. Our next option: in vitro fertilization (IVF), though we weren't sold on that procedure.

"I got a lump in my throat and a pit in my stomach," Marlene said later when our options came down to IVF. "I had a bad feeling. I knew they'd try to harvest as many eggs as possible and make embryos. I just thought, knowing me, that I would get pregnant the first time with quadruplets, and then what would I do with all these remaining embryos? I had that fear from the beginning."

She broached the question with her friend and colleague Brenda.

"Maybe you could get another Christian couple to take them," Brenda said.

Seeds are planted in a variety of ways.

Then came a gloomy morning in January of 1997, the gray sky reflecting our mood. Marlene and I had an appointment with our fertility doctor in San Diego. We were nearing wit's end. In vitro fertilization, we learned at that appointment, was not to become an option for us. The doctor politely explained that Marlene had premature ovarian failure, that pregnancy was not going to happen. The news was devastating. I was forty-four, Marlene thirty-seven. Time, for wannabe parents, was not on our side. What now?

Marlene, tears streaming down her face, recalled her conversation with Brenda.

"Do you have any embryos we could adopt?" she asked the doctor.

This was the first time the words *embryo* and *adopt* were mentioned together.

In vitro fertilization had allowed thousands of couples to conceive and complete their families, but in the process, far more embryos had been created than couples could use once their families were complete. Too many doctors viewed—and still view—IVF as a business transaction. You want a baby, they'll virtually assure you one by producing as many embryos as they can to increase the odds, without considering the ethics of doing so. Hence, there were hundreds of thousands of embryos in frozen storage around the world.

Our doctor discussed with us our options, which revolved around the word *donor*. He suggested using donor eggs, but we considered that option unacceptable. Using donor eggs would represent the creation of life outside a marriage bond. He suggested frozen embryos from a donor. This was already being done, but it did not sit well with us, for several reasons. Couples anonymously donate their remaining embryos to a doctor who essentially is the ultimate authority on what is done with the embryos. We would know nothing about them other than maybe their hair and eye colors. "This is how you choose a car. This is not how we are going to grow our family," Marlene said.

There are no screenings of the couples receiving the donated embryos, no home studies or background checks, as there would be in a traditional adoption. Moreover, these are lives, created at conception, and should not be treated as property. You donate money, food, clothing, time, but you don't donate life.

We had officially arrived at our destination. We were now at wit's end.

The rest of the day was a blur. We had driven in separate cars. Marlene had to report to work immediately following our appointment. I had a pressing deadline on edits for a book I was writing on Tiger Woods and was headed home to work on them. When we reconvened at home later that day, we began discussing other options, including traditional adoption. However, Marlene's desire to experience pregnancy, a baby's first kick, and nursing a newborn was overwhelming, and she continued to return to the idea of adopting frozen embryos.

Adoption of this sort had never been done before. Was it even feasible? That was one question. Another more important one: Would doing so be acceptable in the eyes of God? Those who eventually provided the answers to both questions formed the foundation of our eventual belief that God was working in our lives and that this was his plan.

❄

Early in our marriage, we were living in Irvine, California, where we attended Shepherd of Peace Lutheran Church. Shepherd of Peace was part of the Lutheran Church Missouri Synod (LCMS), of which both of us had been members from birth. The church was less than two miles from Concordia University Irvine, one of several universities around the country that were part of the LCMS. Many of the faculty members at Concordia also were members at Shepherd of Peace, including Concordia's founder, the Rev. Dr. Charles Manske, and Pastor Robert Dargatz, a professor of religion. They and their wives, Barbara Manske and Mary Dargatz, soon became our good friends. We eventually moved to Diamond Bar, California, then to Vista in North San Diego County, but we kept in contact socially with the Manskes and Dargatzes, unaware that eventually they would factor into our embryo adoption story.

The first calls Marlene made in the wake of the devastating news from our fertility doctor were to Pastor Manske and Pastor Dargatz to pose the question: What would God think about our adopting frozen embryos? These men were pillars of our church body and better equipped than anyone we knew to provide answers. Pastor Manske had earned his PhD in social ethics from the University of Southern California and later taught ethics at Concordia. Pastor Dargatz was on the Commission on Theology and Church Relations at the LCMS headquarters in St. Louis, and informed Marlene that the commission was in the process of publishing a document called *Procreative Choices: How Do God's Chosen Choose?*

The document did not discuss placing frozen embryos for adoption, simply because the subject had never before been raised. Nonetheless, Pastor Dargatz introduced Marlene to Rev. Dr. Sam Nafzger, the executive director of the commission. Marlene was in frequent contact with Rev. Nafzger, who was on board with what we wanted to do. "It is a wonderful opportunity that you have been given to lead the way in these new areas of reproductive technologies on the basis of the principles laid down in Holy Scripture," he wrote in a letter to us.

There was one more Christian source from whom Marlene wished to solicit an opinion. When she dialed the phone number, it set in motion a process that would help change not only our lives but the lives of thousands of others.

Every workday morning at seven-thirty, on her commute from Vista to San Diego, Marlene listened to Dr. James Dobson's radio show. Dr. Dobson, the son and grandson of Church of the Nazarene pastors, was the founder of the Christ-centered Focus on the Family and a psychologist with a PhD in child development from the University of Southern California. Marlene decided to reach out for help from Focus on the Family. She phoned its headquarters in Colorado Springs on Friday, January 24, 1997, three days before our twelfth anniversary.

"My husband and I want to adopt frozen embryos remaining from other couples' infertility treatments, and we want to know what God would think about that," she said to the person who answered the phone.

She was politely transferred to a counselor, to whom she repeated her question. Marlene could hear the counselor typing on a computer, and when she was unable to find an answer, she transferred Marlene to a chaplain. She could hear him typing too, and again no answer was forthcoming. By now Marlene was in tears. Finally, almost in desperation, she asked, "Is there any way Dr. Dobson would answer this question for us?"

The chaplain put Marlene on hold while he contacted Dr. Dobson's secretary. When he came back on the line, he said, "Dr. Dobson will be in his office on Monday. If you can get him a letter by Monday, we'll see if he can answer it."

In those days, Dr. Dobson—via his books, radio shows, and ministry at Focus on the Family—was at the height of his extraordinary popularity at home and abroad, and was among the preeminent Christian leaders in the nation. Focus on the Family received thousands of letters and phone calls each week from those seeking answers to difficult questions and help with any number of issues in their lives, and it employed a large trained staff to deal with them. For anyone without a prior relationship with him, the odds of reaching Dr. Dobson himself, though perhaps not on a scale of holding a winning lottery ticket, were exceedingly long.

Marlene is not a gambler, but she placed her bet anyway. She wrote the following letter, dated January 24, 1997, and sent it via FedEx on Saturday the 25th.

Dear Dr. Dobson,

My name is Marlene Strege and I have been a great fan and supporter of Focus for many years. Today, I spoke to your chaplain regarding a situation that my husband and I are involved in. Because of its complexity, we thought you could shed some light on it.

My husband and I will have been married for 12 years this Monday and have been trying to have children, but have been unsuccessful. We started fertility treatments beginning last year. . . . We tried artificial insemination many times as well as fertility drugs for myself, including Metrodin. However, I did not respond to these as hoped with regards to increased egg production with higher doses.

After much prayerful consideration, we decided to go ahead with in vitro fertilization. . . . Last week, after completing our final tests for in vitro, our doctor informed John and me that my FSH [follicle-stimulating hormone] level was very high, which would indicate that I am no longer producing quality eggs. It was too unbearable for us to hear.

Marlene explained everything we had gone through, including options offered by our fertility doctor, among them using donor eggs. Her letter continues:

After much thought, these did not seem like viable choices. However, there is a couple the doctor knew of that had their family through in vitro and they are willing to donate the remaining frozen embryos to a couple.

John and I feel this would be similar to adopting, except at an earlier stage of development than most people adopt. I wish there was a place in the Bible I could go to look up answers to complex situations like this. I have longed to know what it's like to feel a baby's first kick, or to nurse a baby. . . .

Dr. Dobson, how do you think you would answer the questions I've raised? I listen to your program regularly and trust your judgment. To my knowledge, I don't think you've addressed this issue of possible "adoption" of embryos.

You probably don't respond to letters often; I know you are extremely busy. I hope you find it in your heart to drop me a line. Thank you so much for listening to me!

Several days passed, and it began to seem as though the letter was for naught. Then on the following Saturday, the phone rang and Marlene answered.

"Hello, is this Mrs. Streeg, Marlene Streeg?" the caller asked.

"Strege," Marlene replied, correcting the pronunciation (STRAY-gee, hard G).

"Boy, did I mess up that name," the caller said. "Does my voice sound familiar?"

Her immediate thought, oddly, was that someone from the University of Southern California, her alma mater, was calling to solicit a donation.

"Dr. Dobson?" she finally said, incredulously. She was surprised that he was calling, that he was doing so directly rather than having his secretary make the call, and that he was doing so on a Saturday.

They talked for several minutes, and he explained to her that he had never been asked this question and had sought counsel himself. He said he had consulted a pastor; a board member of Focus on the Family; and Dr. Joe McIlhaney, a devout Christian who was among his legion of advisers and a frequent radio guest. Dr. McIlhaney, a gynecologist and infertility specialist based in Austin, Texas, had also been an adviser on social issues to then Texas governor George W. Bush.

Dr. Dobson had initially been skeptical about what we were proposing and expressed his concerns. Dr. McIlhaney, who later became our friend (and my occasional golf partner), asked Dr. Dobson a pointed rhetorical question.

"Jim," he said, "what will happen to those embryos if they are not adopted?"

With that, Dr. Dobson's skepticism vanished. He was on board. He explained to Marlene during their phone conversation that, although he couldn't speak for God, he believed it would be acceptable to adopt frozen embryos from another couple with these caveats:

- None would be selectively aborted when multiple babies resulted from an embryo transfer.
- The parties would be tested for STDs prior to any transfer.
- No more than three embryos at a time would be transferred.

Later that year, in his book *Solid Answers*, Dr. Dobson addressed the issue in greater detail, including a fourth caveat, that "an attorney should handle the relinquishing of rights" by the placing couple as well as overseeing the formal adoption process.[1]

"I would tend to see the option you've been offered as 'adoption' at an earlier stage of development," he wrote. "For an infertile couple such as yourselves to participate in this type of procedure may not be a violation of God's law. From a theological standpoint, I believe the fertilized eggs in question already have an eternal soul (which occurred at the moment of fertilization). . . . By implanting them, you would merely be rescuing embryos that have no other possibility of life."[2]

Dr. Dobson had echoed the conclusions we had received from Pastors Manske, Dargatz, and Nafzger that God very likely would approve of embryo adoption. The theological question answered, two more questions awaited us: How do we go about this, and how do we connect with couples willing to put their frozen embryos up for adoption rather than donation?

They were complicated questions only to us. The answers came without a great deal of difficulty, again an early indication to us that God had his own plan for us—that we needed to "walk by faith, not by sight," as Paul noted in his second letter to the Corinthians, and that God was working in our lives.

CHAPTER 2

Pollyanna

HANNAH'S STORY BEGAN decades before there was a Hannah. It involved a businessman who went to law school despite his low motivation to become an attorney, who took the bar exam on a whim with no expectation of passing it, and who inadvertently became a practicing attorney when he agreed to defend fellow church members sued for protesting outside massage parlors fronting for prostitution. His name is Ron Stoddart, and he is a bona fide hero of our story.

Ron and his wife, Linda, and their children were members of the church Marlene and I attended as kids, Trinity Lutheran in Whittier, California. Marlene occasionally babysat their kids and was part of the youth group that the Stoddarts led. The Stoddarts were high school sweethearts who had mapped out their future together while sitting on the lawn at El Rancho High School in Pico Rivera, California. "We'd sit and talk about how when we got out of high school we'd get married, we'd have a boy, we'd have a girl, then we'd adopt a baby," Ron said. "And the reason we wanted to adopt was because of some families at Pico Baptist church that were adoptive parents, and we just thought they were the greatest parents, the most loving, and we wanted to be like that." This was precisely how the Stoddarts' lives played out. They had two kids, a boy and a girl, then adopted two more.

Ron, meanwhile, had become an executive vice president of a medical supply company. He was also attending law school, though he had "no strong desire to be an attorney." He took the bar exam with no intention of practicing law in the unlikely event that he passed—which somehow he did. "That was a case when God showed me there had to be a use for this."

He appeared in court once and, with an ease that surprised him, got the case against those protesting the massage parlors thrown out of court.

On that day, Ron became an attorney. "That was my trial by fire," he said. "I think from that I came away with the feeling that I don't have to be very smart. I don't have to be eloquent. All I have to be is available. From that, I believed that practicing law is not brain surgery. It's just arguing. And the most important part was to know what you believe, know what your position is, and if it's something you really believe, it's not going to be hard."

Still, Ron immediately tabled his law career and went back to work at Omnimedical. He stayed on even after the company had gone public, until health issues intervened. When he eventually returned to work, it occurred to him that this was not how he wished to spend his life: checking the stock price every morning, concerned with how much money he might make.

So he resigned and took a year off. Then his pastor called with a request. The pastor had friends who needed help completing an adoption, and he knew Ron was an attorney and adoptive parent. Ron had never been on the attorney side of an adoption, but he agreed to help anyway.

The adopting couple soon introduced Ron to a pastor in Beverly Hills, California. The pastor, who was actively involved with Lutheran Church Missouri Synod pro-life causes, asked Ron to help him with the maternity homes (now called crisis pregnancy centers) that he had leased from the Department of Housing and Urban Development. Ron agreed. This led to his assisting in adoptions for several other couples. However, the money he had made from selling his Omnimedical stock was dwindling quickly.

He turned to prayer. "Okay, God, if you want me to keep doing this, show me how I can at least take a salary."

A week or so later his prayer was answered. He received a phone call from the founder of House of Ruth, a ministry of Calvary Chapel in Downey, California. She was looking for a Christian attorney to handle its adoptions. Ron accepted the offer and went from doing four or five adoptions a year to doing fifty, then one hundred.

This led to his accepting a position as executive director of Christian Adoptions and Family Services (formerly named the Evangelical Welfare Association of Whittier and later known as Nightlight Christian Adoptions). This, incidentally, was the agency through which Dr. James Dobson and his wife, Shirley, had adopted their son, and Pastor Manske and wife, Barbara, had adopted two of their three children.

Ron's journey from businessman to adoption attorney was not a coincidence, although he had not foreseen or pursued it. "This was God's plan," he said. "I never really thought about using my law degree to do adoptions until I started working with the Lutheran pastor."

Over the years, we had lost touch with Ron and Linda. We had not seen them since our wedding in 1985, though we were aware he was working in adoptions. In the wake of our infertility diagnosis, Marlene called him, and we arranged to meet him on February 5, 1997, at Coco's Bakery Restaurant in Brea, California.

When we arrived at Coco's, we proceeded to a booth, and Ron patiently walked us through our two options—domestic or international adoption. He explained that we *would* be parents; it was not a matter of if but of when and how. When he had finished, Marlene introduced a third *how*.

"Ron, we want to adopt frozen embryos," she said.

Ron obviously knew what an embryo is, but he was not attuned to what was happening with infertility treatments and the excessive number of embryos created and in frozen storage. But as Marlene was explaining, Ron was recalling pieces of a story from England about embryos frozen for several years that were going to be destroyed. Thousands of them—three thousand, in fact—had been in frozen storage for more than five years. They were facing destruction according to British law limiting the length of time unclaimed frozen embryos could be maintained.

"I remembered hearing that and thinking, 'That's wrong. That's an embryo. That's life,'" Ron said. The news coverage had gone on to another topic, and Ron gave it no further thought—until Marlene began talking about frozen embryos.

There was no logical reason Ron should have agreed to help us do what had never been done and what was certain to be complicated and time consuming. He was an exceedingly busy man, frequently traveling abroad to facilitate adoptions of Russian orphans. Our request was a headache waiting to happen. Yet Ron never hesitated—never so much as flinched—when Marlene asked him if we could do this.

"Of course we can," he said.

I asked him several years later why he so eagerly agreed to help us when other adoption agencies almost certainly would have declined.

"I think it would have been because people think inside the box, that you can't adopt a baby from a pregnant woman until the baby has been born," he said, noting what should be obvious to all, that life begins at conception.

There was one other factor. At Ron's first job out of college, working for the City of Los Angeles, his nickname in his division was Pollyanna. "I've always seen the bright side of things," he said. He is the proverbial glass-half-full, a perpetual and infectious optimist who simply was responding according to his nature and his love of children.

Ron became a vital advocate on our behalf. It was our desire, and his, to have embryo adoption treated the same as traditional open adoptions, the only difference being that they occur at an earlier stage. But there were additional challenges, and Ron needed help.

He turned to JoAnn Davidson, also known as J. D. (and now by her married name, JoAnn Eiman), who had joined Nightlight Christian Adoptions to do birth-mother outreach.

"What do you think about embryos?" Ron asked her one day.

"I think they're babies," J. D. replied.

"Well, what do you think about adopting embryos?" Ron asked her.

"Somebody ought to be doing it," J. D. replied.

"Well, how about we do it?" Ron said.

This was how Nightlight's embryo adoption program began, without a name. Ron asked J. D. to develop a program.

"I didn't know what IVF meant," she said years later. "I knew nothing about artificial insemination or in vitro or any of those concepts. So I started going to conferences or gatherings where they disseminate information and started sitting in all these talks to would-be patients. And I'd start looking up a bunch of words. What does *in vitro* mean— test tube or petri dish? I hear IVF, I thought it meant in a petri dish when it really meant outside the body.

"I had to learn about a whole new language. I had to learn, Can you ship an embryo, and how do you do that? There was a huge learning curve. Then Ron and I stared at each other. Where do we get an embryo?"

The program she and Ron developed was similar to those that facilitate traditional adoptions. It included everything from background checks and blood work to legal documents.

"I think I saw in my life the Lord working through me, using me in my vocation, more so than any other job I'd ever had," J. D. said. "It was a job unlike any other. It was always new. How do you handle this family selection? How do you handle contracts? How do you handle the families, the doctors? God was using me. I absolutely believe it was a team effort, people in my office supporting me, supporting Ron, who I think is a genius.

"One of the things that stuck with me is that he always wanted to share our program. He said, 'This isn't our program. If any adoption agency wants to know about this, we're going to help them and teach them for free. We want more babies to be saved.' It wasn't exclusive to us. That amazed me. He wasn't motivated by fame or money. This was his true heart. It didn't matter as long as children were saved from destruction."

We could not have asked for a better team to work on our behalf, and later on behalf of so many others, than Ron, J. D., and the rest of the staff at Nightlight Christian Adoptions.

Still, at this—dare I say it?—embryonic stage of this embryo adoption program, the prevailing question lingered: *Where do we find embryos?*

CHAPTER 3

Snowflakes

ALL OF US want life to unfold according to our own script and timing, forgetting the Proverbs 3:5 directive to "trust in the LORD with all your heart and lean not on your own understanding." Marlene and I weren't watching the clock so much as we were watching the calendar. Months were passing, not hours, and though we seemed to have everything in place, we were missing something.

Embryos and a doctor to transfer them.

It was a stressful time in our lives. We were concerned not only with how this might play out and the possibility that it might not play out in our favor but also with the outcome of a job interview I had recently had with *Golf Digest*. There was the looming possibility that I might be making a job change after nineteen years as a sportswriter for the *Orange County Register*.

We needed a vacation. We chose to go to Colorado—first to Colorado Springs to pay a visit to Focus on the Family, hoping for a meeting with Dr. Dobson, followed by several days at bed-and-breakfasts in Breckenridge.

The morning after our arrival in Colorado Springs, we went straight to Focus on the Family's headquarters, a beautiful campus at the northern end of town with Pikes Peak as a backdrop. Dr. Dobson's assistant had arranged for us to view a taping of Dr. Dobson's radio show, this one on clergy appreciation. At its conclusion, Dr. Dobson said, "Are John and Marlene Strege in the audience?" We were not expecting that.

We were escorted into the studio for a brief visit with Dr. Dobson, then invited up to his office. We met with him for nearly half an hour. After a discussion about USC football—both he and Marlene have degrees from USC, and he and I share an interest in its football program—he asked whether he had adequately addressed our question in his newest book, *Solid Answers*. He had addressed it perfectly.

Dr. Dobson had arranged for us to have lunch with Sydna Massé, who was the crisis pregnancy director for Focus, and a man from their physicians' outreach program. We were mystery guests to them; Dr. Dobson had said only that we'd tell them what we were doing. The lunch lasted two hours. We discussed what we were attempting to do, and we had an attentive and appreciative audience.

We then went with Sydna to her desk, and she presented Marlene with a baby blanket. She told us later that after we left, she had said a brief prayer: "That is really cool, God. Let me help them. Let me be part of that."

The next day Marlene and I drove to Breckenridge. We had a memorable time that included a stay in a remote bed-and-breakfast on the Continental Divide and a wilderness walk with a llama carrying our lunches. The llama, however, got loose and stubbornly resisted our efforts to catch it, remaining in our sight but out of reach. In hindsight, it sufficed as a metaphor for our own journey. We could envision where we wanted to go, but getting there remained elusive.

We returned to Colorado Springs for our flight home, but before we left, Marlene had a gift for Sydna and phoned ahead to ask whether we could stop by. One of Sydna's associates answered the phone, and though we had not met, she seemed to know who we were and why we were there.

"Oh, so you heard what we're trying to do," Marlene said to her.

"Yes," she replied sweetly. "God must have thought you were special to have chosen you to do this."

Wow. The notion that we might have been chosen had not occurred

to us. We simply wanted a baby, and this was the route we had prayerfully opted to take.

❄

We returned home and began the wait anew. Marlene met with Ron
Stoddart and got an update on how things were progressing on his end.
It was then that we learned that when a couple gave us their frozen
embryo, it would not be legally recognized by the state as an adoption.
Sadly, though not surprisingly, embryos are considered to be property,
not people. Still, Ron insisted the process be treated in the same manner
as a traditional adoption. We had to go through background checks,
a home study, meetings with social workers, blood tests, and a CPR
certification course for me. (Marlene's job as an occupational therapist
already required her to have CPR certification.)

"We completed all of the requirements for adoption for the State
of California even though legally we did not have to," Marlene noted
later. "However, birth moms do not donate the child they are pregnant
with, and countries do not donate orphans from their countries. So why
would this be different?"

During her meeting with Ron, he referred to these embryos in storage as residing in "frozen orphanages." That was the first time we heard
the phrase. As usual, Ron had the right words, and he remained fully
committed.

Still, we had bouts of concern, unsure what we had gotten into and
where it was headed. "Sometimes," Marlene wrote in her journal, "I get
scared because it's all so new. Jesus, please give me strength and courage
to continue."

Those supporting us never wavered, for which we are ever grateful.
Pastor Manske always listened attentively and made copies of whatever
documents we had, while remaining upbeat and encouraging. His wife,
Barbara, summed it up neatly to Marlene. "This whole thing—the

Tiger book, the [potential] baby, John's job interview—it's like a tapestry, each little bit is its own thread in the tapestry."

My book on Tiger Woods, published a few weeks after he won the Masters by twelve shots in April 1997, had provided us the means to cover whatever future costs we might incur with embryo transfers and such. It was one small part of a larger puzzle in which pieces kept falling into place, even though we still had no embryos.

In early October, at the invitation of our neighbor, Marlene attended a women's weekend retreat. The musical guest was Teresa Muller, a well-known Christian singer whom Marlene admired so much that she had presented Dr. Dobson with one of her albums. Marlene introduced herself to Teresa and told her about giving Dr. Dobson the CD, though she explained she was presently unable to reveal why we had met with him.

Teresa replied that it was okay—she respected Marlene's need to keep her reasons private, just as Jesus's mother, Mary, had kept her pregnancy to herself at first. It wasn't for her to tell; it was for the angels. Teresa stressed how Mary had "kept all these things and pondered them in her heart" (Luke 2:19 NKJV).

Marlene's jaw dropped and tears began to stream down her cheeks. "It's amazing you would use that exact example," she said to Teresa. "What prompted you to say that?"

"God impressed upon me to tell you that," she said. "I have no idea why, but these must have been the right words at the right time, based on your tears."

The words indeed were timely. "Once again," Marlene wrote in her journal when she had returned home, "I see God's fingerprints on the events of my life."

❊

Later that month, our fertility doctor let us down. He had not responded to a letter Ron Stoddart had written to him explaining our desire to adopt frozen embryos and asking his help in connecting us with the genetic parents of frozen embryos. When Marlene finally called him, the nurse told her the doctor had received Ron's information but was not interested in participating in the program. He declined to give a reason, and the matter was not open for discussion. We learned later that he was concerned he might eventually be sued for being responsible for the genetic material. It was an odd posture to take for a doctor who dealt with genetic material daily.

Another setback. Why, Lord?

As Dr. Dobson explained in his book *When God Doesn't Make Sense*, "He does not explain Himself to man. We *can* say with confidence that while His purposes and plans are very different from ours, He is infinitely just and His timing is always perfect. He intervenes at just the right moment for our ultimate good. Until we hear from Him, then, we would be wise not to get in a lather."[1]

Ron was concerned we might be getting in "a lather." He called that evening and said we all needed to avoid knee-jerk reactions to every development and instead take a deep breath while we considered our options. He suggested we brainstorm ideas on the weekend. When the weekend arrived, Ron, J. D., and Marlene met and went over a list of doctors. J. D. had begun arranging appointments for Ron to meet with the doctors.

Meanwhile, Marlene had called Dr. Dobson's office one Friday, seeking his opinion. His secretary sensed that Marlene was somewhat distraught that day. Early the following week, Dr. Dobson phoned her and said he'd heard she hadn't been doing well. He relayed that he was going to ask a doctor friend of his about the possible availability of frozen embryos at Johns Hopkins Hospital. He also intended to raise the issue at Focus on the Family's physicians' conference, specifically with the Physicians Resource Council, in November. He also reminded Marlene that God was still in control.

Marlene's entry in her journal, dated November 28, 1997: "I just read my Bible lesson. Today it said, 'defend orphans.' Isaiah 1:17."

Three days later, Willy Wooten, director of counseling at Focus on the Family, received a phone call from a wonderful Christian woman who had gone through in vitro fertilization and had triplets. She and her husband had embryos remaining in frozen storage, and, grounded in the Christian belief that life begins at conception, they knew they could not simply have them destroyed. More concerned than desperate, though understandably anxious, she was asking if there was anyone who might be able to take them.

When they finished the call, Wooten went straight to Sydna Massé. "I've got something that's going to stump you," he said.

Or not.

Wooten explained the call he had received. Sydna took the woman's phone number and immediately phoned her. The woman explained her dilemma: twenty embryos to place. She obviously couldn't give birth to twenty more children. Could Sydna help?

"I know who the parents are," Sydna replied, recalling our lunch together. It was another *wow* moment in a growing series of them.

By the following morning, Marlene and the woman were on the phone together. As in a traditional adoption, it was the woman and her husband's decision whom to choose as parents. Marlene's bond with the woman strengthened quickly as they continued to have conversations.

There were still obstacles, but finally, against what once seemed insurmountable odds, we had something more than hope.

❋

We can never repay Ron for what he has done for us and has meant to us. But in December 1997, as a small token of our appreciation, we invited him and his wife, Linda, to join us for a Christmas dinner show at the renowned Hotel del Coronado across San Diego Bay from downtown San Diego. The show was called *An American Christmas* and was

staged by the Lamb's Players Theatre in Coronado. The show was set
around 1900, with the actors in full Victorian regalia.

During the program, an actress playing the role of a relative from
Germany lamented that San Diego, unlike her native country, had no
snow at Christmas. Touching the cheek of a little blond-haired girl, she
began a soliloquy about a snowflake:

> *In the intricate design of each flake of snow,*
> *we find the Creator reflecting the individual human heart.*

Ron and Marlene simultaneously looked at one another, eyes wide. It
was a perfect and beautiful description of a frozen embryo. At intermission, Ron turned to the three of us and said, "We now have the name of
our new program. The Snowflakes Embryo Adoption Program."

"Once in a while you hear people say that 'God gave me a word,'"
Ron said years later. "This is the one time in my life when I can really say
God gave us the word. It came from [an actress] who had no idea what
the impact would be or what she was talking about. Talk about God's
perfect plan. Nothing could have been more perfect than Snowflakes
from heaven, frozen. It was amazing. It still gives me chills."

CHAPTER 4

An Easter Pregnancy

ON NEW YEAR'S EVE, 1997, the placing couple made it official: They had read our home study, had gotten to know us via phone conversations and letters, and had chosen us to adopt their twenty remaining embryos. Ron Stoddart had received the good news and phoned us on New Year's Day to deliver it. "Words cannot express the joy we felt," Marlene wrote in her journal.

Marlene spoke with the woman and detected no remorse. "She said she loved them [the embryos] because they were something God created, but that I was going to be the mother," Marlene wrote. "That made me cry." Their family desired anonymity, a request we honor to this day. We hold them in the highest regard, as we do all those families who had to make the most difficult decision to relinquish their frozen embryos to others.

Five weeks later, the process was proceeding at a glacial pace and frustration had momentarily intruded on our joy. Then this timely Scripture verse turned up: "The vision is yet for an appointed time. . . . Though it tarries, wait for it; because it will surely come" (Hab. 2:3 NKJV).

On February 20, 1998, Marlene began to receive daily injections of progesterone and estrogen in preparation for the transfer of embryos at a Pasadena, California, fertility clinic with a doctor found by Focus on the Family. Two weeks later, the nurse from the fertility clinic called. "The Snowflakes are here," she said.

They had been shipped via FedEx. "Have visions of a guardian angel on FedEx plane with arms around Snowflakes in liquid nitrogen," Marlene wrote.

A day later the embryologist called to say they had thawed twelve embryos, but only three had survived, and only one of the three looked marginally promising. The odds were not in our favor, but still we were hopeful, and we knew God was in control.

Finally, on March 7, we went in for the transfer. The doctor explained that the embryos weren't ideal because of fragmentation occurring during the thaw, but we were excited nonetheless. The doctor showed us a photo of the embryos. "Look at the golf swing on that one," he said jokingly.

Following the transfers, Marlene had to remain lying down for a while, after which we went to lunch. "Remember," I said helpfully (or not), "you're eating for four."

When we got home, we received a phone call from Dr. Dobson. "He said everyone was praying for us. He's unbelievable!" Marlene said.

Then the waiting began. We would not know for another twelve days or so whether any of the embryos had implanted. The range of emotions tilted toward depressing: maybe it wasn't happening; maybe it was never going to happen. Our friend Dot Mericle—a surrogate mother of sorts to Marlene after the death of her own mother, Eileen, twenty years earlier—suggested that Marlene visualize a box, put all her worries in it, wrap it with a pretty bow, and hand it over to Jesus.

That part worked. But alas, the embryos did not implant, and Marlene was not pregnant. "I find comfort in knowing that these little ones have been released from their frozen state and are in the arms of our heavenly Father," Marlene wrote.

She resumed the injections, and her doctor noticed her uterine lining was two centimeters thicker than it had been previously, a good sign. On Good Friday, the remaining eight embryos were thawed. Three survived, and two of the three were "excellent," we were told.

The following day we went in for the transfer, this time by a different doctor. He showed us a photo of the embryos taken the previous day when they were thawed, and another taken shortly before our arrival. The second photo showed that the embryos had already advanced to their next stage of development.

Before the doctor began the transfer, Marlene asked if she could pray with him. "Absolutely," he said, bowing his head and folding his hands.

"Heavenly Father, we acknowledge that you alone are the Creator of all life." She then asked that God bless the physician and guide his hands and that we would have a successful transfer and ultimately an implantation.

"That was great," the doctor said.

We were hopeful and buoyed by the fact that the transfer had been made on Easter weekend, with its promise of new life.

The Sunday after Easter, I left for San Francisco to research a story on the Olympic Club there, which was to host the U.S. Open in June.

"I was in bed and looking at the stars," Marlene wrote while I was gone. "A thought came to me that God had come through each time, whenever there was a setback, and had done something so great, and I thought, 'If this doesn't work, then God has something even more wonderful planned.' I felt so much peace about that and thanked God for that thought."

On Monday, Marlene's nurse phoned to say that, based on her most recent blood test, her hCG (human chorionic gonadotropin, the pregnancy hormone) was fifty-seven and that "something is going on." She asked that Marlene keep it between the two of us, so of course Marlene told everyone we knew, or so it seemed—though she had a reason for doing so beyond her excitement: they might pray for us and the embryos.

On Tuesday, Marlene had blood work done again.

On Wednesday, she went to the crisis pregnancy center to see a friend who worked there, Dana Chisholm. My wife told her that her period was two days late. "Let's go take a pregnancy test," Dana said. The test turned out positive. Fingers were crossed and prayers were said.

On Thursday, Marlene met a friend for lunch at the Disneyland Hotel. She phoned her nurse from there.

"Congratulations," Marlene's nurse said. "You're pregnant!"

She went on to tell Marlene about testing and assorted other topics. Marlene heard none of it.

"I'm sorry," she said, "could you repeat what you just said?"

"You're pregnant!"

"I got that part," Marlene replied. "It was everything you said after that."

The rest of the afternoon remained a blur for Marlene. I, as yet unaware of the news, was flying home that evening. Marlene was picking me up at the airport, and when I deplaned, I spotted her off in the distance, holding three white roses tied together with blue and pink ribbons. I gave her a thumbs-up. Elation cannot adequately describe our emotions that day.

By the following morning, the news had reached all the way to Europe. Ron Stoddart called from Frankfurt, Germany, to congratulate us. Even he began crying. He was personally invested and as happy and emotional as we were. A few days later, a dozen red roses arrived at the house, sent by Dr. Dobson and his wife, Shirley. The outpouring of love and support from friends old and new, near and far, was humbling.

※

In early May, Marlene's doctor did an ultrasound and saw one baby. The doctor was thrilled.

"It was a textbook implantation," he said.

"Of course it was," Marlene said. "God doesn't do second best."

The following day, Marlene went to Nightlight Christian Adoptions' offices, where lunch was delivered for the crew. They had a baby pool on the number of babies and the due date. The winner, Cami, had predicted one baby and a January 1, 1999, due date. The due date, in fact, was January 2. (I joked that I preferred the baby to check in three days earlier for tax purposes.)

In late July, Marlene bought maternity clothes for the first time, even wearing one of the outfits out of the store. When she caught a silhouette of herself in a window, she began to cry. "I never thought that as an adoptive mom I would be buying maternity clothes for myself," she said.

The months that followed were nothing out of the ordinary, a good thing with a pregnancy. Marlene had morning sickness frequently in the first trimester and was hungry at odd hours in the third trimester, often in the middle of the night. She kept a box of saltine crackers by the bed and shared them with our dog, Chelsea, a gleeful accomplice in Marlene's midnight cravings.

Marlene was given three baby showers—one by friends at work, another by her sister, and a third by our neighbor. They were spoiling her, and she loved it all, these celebrations of what was to come.

Shortly before midnight, on December 30, 1998, Marlene's water broke and mayhem ensued, though not for the typical reasons. Marlene, no longer willing to navigate the stairs in the final days of her pregnancy, had taken to sleeping on the pullout couch in the family room while I slept upstairs. So when her water broke, she went to the bottom of the stairs and began shouting to wake me up. She was yelling, Chelsea was barking, and I was still asleep. Finally she got Chelsea to run up the stairs barking, and I awoke and called the doctor.

We were instructed to head to the Mary Birch Hospital for Women and Newborns at Sharp Memorial Hospital in San Diego, about a forty-five-minute drive. We arrived around 2:00 a.m. to find no room available—"no room in the inn," Marlene said, maintaining her sense of humor. Neither was a nurse available to care for Marlene. She waited in triage until a room finally opened around 4:00 a.m. An ultrasound showed that the baby was wedged in sideways, so a doctor recommended a C-section (likely sparing me the embarrassment of revealing that I remembered nothing from our childbirth classes). One final obstacle: the operating schedule for that day was already full. So the C-section had to be done immediately.

At seven minutes after 7:00 a.m. on December 31, 1998, Hannah Eileen Strege introduced herself to the world.

❄

"You were perfect," Marlene wrote of our newborn. "I remember when they carried you from me to the warming table you looked at Daddy and me with this perfect little 'O' mouth open! You were so beautiful."

Six pounds, fourteen ounces and seventeen inches long, Hannah was "petite, like her father," I said. Later that day, we celebrated with a hospital toast—sparkling cider in champagne flutes with snowflakes etched on them.

Incidentally, we chose the name Hannah when we learned that it loosely translates to "gift from God." She certainly was that. And Eileen, the name of Marlene's late mother, paid homage to the grandmother Hannah would not meet until our ultimate reunion in heaven. We agreed that Hannah Eileen sounded good together.

What a journey it had been from where we started. Two years of wildly shifting emotions and wondering where it all was headed . . . twenty embryos in frozen storage, shipped just ten months ago to California via FedEx, one resulting in a birth . . .

We not only called our new daughter Hannah Eileen, we also called her our miracle baby.

CHAPTER 5

Hannah's First Radio Show

THE NEXT FEW months likely were similar to the early months of parenthood for any couple—an enormous adjustment, a steep learning curve on caring for a newborn, and, initially, a lack of sleep, all of it infused with euphoria over the blessing that had taken over our lives. The learning curve included our giving Hannah her first bath *after* we had fed her rather than before, resulting in her spitting up her food—a rookie mistake on our part.

Marlene's meticulous notes, meanwhile, included Hannah having "watched her first golf tournament with Daddy (Mercedes Championship)" on January 9, "watched her first Super Bowl" on January 24, and "first time to Nordstrom with Mommy" on February 28. On the Nordstrom front, it would not be the last time, I noted wryly. Then there was this, the good Lord showing compassion for older first-time parents: "Slept 9–6!" on March 3, 4, and 5. She was sleeping through the night at two months, though not everyone shared in our joy at this. At the reunion of the parents from our birthing classes, we were asked how the babies were sleeping. The couples went around the room telling their horror stories and then it came to us. "Sleeping through the night at two months," I said, eliciting a chorus of boos from an unappreciative audience.

The highlight of those early months was Hannah's baptism on April 24, 1999, at Good Shepherd Chapel, a beautiful, small sanctuary on the campus of Concordia University Irvine atop a hillside with expansive views of Orange County. We chose this site out of appreciation for the counsel we had received from the founder of the university, our friend the Rev. Dr. Charles Manske, who also conducted the service and performed the baptism.

It was fitting that Pastor Manske, whose mandate in founding Concordia was honoring the Great Commission, included it in the responsive reading:

Pastor: The nature of baptism.
People: What is baptism?
Pastor: Baptism is not simple water only, but it is the water comprehended in God's command and connected with God's Word.
People: What is that Word of God?
Pastor: Christ, our Lord, says in the last chapter of Matthew: "Go ye into all the world and teach all nations, baptizing them in the name of the Father, and of the Son, and of the Holy Spirit."

We asked our friends Pastor Robert and Mary Dargatz to serve as Hannah's sponsors, and Pastor Dargatz also was responsible for the Scripture readings. Both of the readings spoke to us then and continue to do so today.

Before I formed you in the womb I knew you, before you were born I set you apart; I appointed you as a prophet to the nations. (Jer. 1:5)

"I prayed for this child, and the LORD has granted me what I asked of him. So now I give him to the LORD. For his whole life he will be given over to the LORD." (1 Sam. 1:27–28)

It was a family and friends affair, as baptisms generally are. Our neighbor was the soloist and sang "Sleep Sound in Jesus" and "Masterpiece." My brother was the usher. Hannah's cousins were the greeters. My parents were there, as was Marlene's father.

The only way the day could have been better is if Marlene's mother and Hannah's grandmother, Eileen Hoelzel, had been there. She had died from cancer eighteen years earlier. "She would have been the biggest Snowflakes cheerleader," Marlene said later. "She would have loved the Snowflakes movement—and her granddaughter."

We honored her at Hannah's baptism by including a single rose in loving memory.

In mid-May our relationship with Dr. Dobson and his wife, Shirley, resumed for reasons we could not yet envision. Marlene was invited to attend Focus on the Family's Renewing the Heart women's ministries conference at what then was called the Arrowhead Pond (now the Honda Center) in Anaheim. Mrs. Dobson was one of the featured speakers. The night before the conference, Marlene and I were invited to a reception at the Arrowhead Pond, and we met up with the Dobsons.

At the end of the month, when Hannah was five months old, we took her to Colorado Springs and Focus on the Family. We renewed our friendship with Sydna Massé, one of the key players in our connecting with the genetic parents, and introduced her to Hannah.

The next day we met with Dr. Dobson, followed by our first radio broadcast with him. On that initial broadcast, we used the pseudonyms Elizabeth and Zach, and Hannah was referred to as Grace. Our families and friends knew of Hannah's origins, and though we never attempted to hide her story, we also never intended to tell her story publicly, since at the time there was no reason to do so.

Also on the broadcast with us were Dr. Joe McIlhaney, Ron Stoddart, and Sydna. Dr. Dobson walked us through our story, from the heartbreak of infertility to the joy that was Hannah. The heartbreak was still vivid in Marlene's mind. She noted how, in the years before Hannah was born, she would not go to church on Mother's Day.

"My mother had passed away. I had no mother, and I wasn't a mother," Marlene said. "Church services on Mother's Day are geared toward mothers. It was difficult for me to go, so I stopped going to church on Mother's Day."[1]

Dr. Dobson asked her how long she had wanted a baby. "As long as I can remember," she said. Even as a little girl? "Oh, yeah, absolutely."

He inquired about her yearning to get pregnant. "You want a baby so bad you will do anything to have a baby. You will spend any cost to have a baby. I have since spoken to one woman who has spent sixty thousand dollars on the infertility process and has not been able to conceive a child, and that's money they didn't have. That was going into their retirement funds."

Dr. McIlhaney had heard that story too many times. "[People] don't understand it," he said. "Our society, as Elizabeth said, is set up to honor mothers and those women who have babies, and if they don't, there must be something wrong with them. I've heard that in my office year after year. I agree with Elizabeth. In my opinion, this is one of the most painful things that can happen, especially to a woman."

Marlene explained, "When we met with the doctor and he informed us that tests showed that we would not be able to have our own genetic child, it just hit me like a ton of bricks. It meant something different for me. For me it meant that I would not be able to experience pregnancy. I would not be able to feel a baby's kick or to feel a baby growing in me. I had wanted to feel that for so long, even morning sickness, even the downside. God *wants* you to have children. I wanted to do all those things. I just remember walking out and I was just in tears.

"Everyone says you can always adopt. I had listened to a Focus broadcast a couple months before, and you had a wonderful call-in show on adoption. I was actually on my way to one of my ultrasound appointments at that point, and I didn't get to hear the whole broadcast, so I called and asked for the tape. That tape came the day before the doctor had told us."

"Just at the right moment," Dr. Dobson said.

"Right. I think God was trying to open my heart toward adoption."

Sydna spoke about the role she played after learning of the call from the woman who wanted to place twenty frozen embryos for adoption.

"By the end of that afternoon, I was talking to that genetic mother," she said. "When I started to describe Elizabeth to her and to say that 'God's hands are already on this,' she said, 'Do you think they want to do this?' I said, 'They've already done all the legal backgrounds and done the ethical checking, and I really do believe they're the parents of your children.'"

Dr. Dobson's thorough debriefing included Ron Stoddart's reasoning for why our situation had to be handled in the same fashion as a traditional adoption. "It is a new frontier," Ron said, "and there are very, very few laws that deal with the rights of embryos or the process for legally transferring embryos. Basically, in the United States, the laws treat embryos as property. To transfer an embryo requires a written agreement or a contract. But it really does not treat them as life. From my earliest conversations with Zach and Elizabeth, we agreed that the only way we would do this is if it was done as an adoption. So Zach and Elizabeth had a home study done, which not only was a legal screening but prepared them for parenting an adopted child."

He described the genetic mother's concerns and how they were similar to concerns he had heard from so many parents placing children for adoption: *These are my children and I want to provide for them. Help me.*

Ron continued, "We tried to create an environment of support, education, protection for the parties by doing this as close to a legal adoption as you can do, considering that the law does not recognize an embryo as an adoptable child."

Dr. Dobson explained how he had reached the conclusion that

adopting frozen embryos was morally acceptable. "After being a family counselor, there aren't many questions I haven't heard one time or another, but this one was new to me," he said. "They asked me if it would be morally right if they could adopt frozen embryos and how I felt about that. I began consulting with other Christian leaders, including Dr. Joe McIlhaney. Finally, I counseled Zach and Elizabeth that I thought it would be a good thing to rescue those little human beings, considering the alternatives. Think about it. If a woman does not give birth to those embryos, they'll eventually be destroyed. We believe that life begins at conception, so this is just adoption at an earlier age. That's the way I see it."

Given our difficulty in locating a fertility doctor willing to do the transfers, Dr. Dobson inquired, how had we eventually found one?

"Actually," Marlene replied, "it was through Focus on the Family again."

"You now know why I'm the godfather of that little baby that's out there," a beaming Dr. Dobson said.

He asked Marlene to read the letter she had written to Hannah's genetic parents, following the protocols that Nightlight Christian Adoptions had in place for adopting couples:

Dear Genetic Family,

We want you to know that we've been praying for you virtually from the moment the idea of embryo adoption was conceived. We understand to a degree the anguish you surely feel over the future of your embryos. When we were pondering in vitro, we were concerned about the fate of the unused embryos—each a son or daughter, a brother or sister.

We understand that these and other embryos around the world are wanted children, wanted by God. That each of them is His gift. One day when the time has come to share with them their remarkable beginnings, we will tell them that God let one family start them and another family complete them. God is good, isn't He?

We have been considering what we may say to you and have concluded that this is what we would have needed to hear had we been in a similar situation: We will do everything in our power to lead these children to Jesus, so that one day all of us will be rejoicing in Heaven. This is our promise to you.

Marlene teared up at the end. "Those tears speak volumes about what this entire experience means to you," Dr. Dobson said. He then asked Sydna to read the letter the genetic parents had sent to us. The last paragraph read:

> Please let any children God brings into this world know we love them dearly. Most importantly, however, we ask that you bring them safely to the waters of Holy Baptism, that you teach them to love Jesus Christ, and to trust Him as their only Lord and Savior.

That was our own mandate as well.

"As we have been talking," Dr. Dobson said near the end of the taping, "Sydna stepped out and brought little Grace into the studio, and here she is."

The crowd viewing the taping of the broadcast from the gallery gave her a sustained ovation.

"Isn't she beautiful?" he said.

"First of all, to Zach and Elizabeth and that precious baby that you're holding in your arms, what a marvelous thing. I am so thrilled to play a tiny role in this, and as I said earlier, I feel like the godfather of this child. May I have that role?"

"Absolutely," Marlene replied.

In closing the broadcast, Dr. Dobson asked important questions,

and Ron Stoddart provided critical answers. Ron's responses spoke to
his unequivocal love for children that drove his passion for adoption—
domestic, international, or embryonic—and confirmed that this passion was not driven by ego or a desire for revenue.

First, Dr. Dobson asked Ron what should be done about these vast
numbers of embryos in frozen orphanages.

"I think it's going to take people of faith to recognize that these are
preborn babies," Ron said. "I just have a tremendous amount of respect
for the genetic mother and father of Grace. [The genetic mother] was so
brave in continuing to seek out God's will and to seek out an answer for
her embryos. I think that's what the women who have frozen embryos
now need to do. They need to understand that these are their children,
and they need to make a plan for them.

"We have a program that we have started that is called Snowflakes,
specifically helping to unite genetic parents with adopting families. I
would encourage genetic parents, regardless where they might live, to
contact a licensed agency because I think they need the formality and
protection and support of adoption professionals as they do this."

Dr. Dobson asked, "Could an attorney out there someplace contact you for a copy of the agreement, so they don't have to start from
scratch?"

"Absolutely," Ron replied. "Attorneys and Christian adoption agencies. I would be happy to share it. Our goal is to see every one of those
embryos have a chance for life."

Dr. Dobson turned to Dr. McIlhaney and asked him what his concerns were.

"My concern is that we stop producing those frozen embryos in excess
of what people want to have put back in their uteruses," he replied.
"Most people going through this process do not know that they can tell
their physicians they do not want all their eggs fertilized. I'm calling
on patients who might go through IVF to talk to their physicians and
not let them fertilize all their eggs unless they intend to come back for

them. If those physicians won't go along with that, go to another clinic and another doctor."

In his closing acknowledgments, Dr. Dobson said, "I want to congratulate Sydna, because if it had not been for your role, there perhaps would have been somebody else involved, but you made it possible."

"Well, the Lord was involved in all this," Sydna replied. "I just got to tag along, which was a blessing."

"Dr. McIlhaney," Dr. Dobson said, "if you had given me the wrong answer on the day that we talked, I would have conveyed that, I'm sure, to this family."

"I think [the answer I gave] was God's plan," Dr. McIlhaney replied.

Dr. Dobson is an avid sports fan, so presumably he will both forgive and appreciate my use of the following cliché, that in this broadcast he "touched 'em all," as the late great broadcaster Dick Enberg would say. He had touched all the bases, expertly and passionately.

❄

This was the first time—but far from the last—that Dr. Dobson would talk about embryo adoption. In so doing, he introduced the concept to the world at large. Given his vast reach—three thousand radio stations and a daily audience upward of 1.5 million in the United States alone—the potential impact cannot be overstated, and it began to play out on the day Focus on the Family aired the show.

"They called us [Nightlight Christian Adoptions] and said, 'We're going to do a [magazine] story on embryo adoption. You'd better be ready, because your phone is going to be ringing off the hook,'" said JoAnn Davidson (J. D.), who was now the director of the Snowflakes Embryo Adoption Program.

Ron Stoddart ordered two new phone lines installed at Nightlight. He also conducted a training session with his staff to prepare them not only for the story in Focus on the Family's magazine but also for the broadcast that would follow. When the story landed, the phones began ringing—"an avalanche," they called it—and continued nonstop through the end of the day. Prior to the Focus article, Nightlight had received 250 inquiries in ten days. When the article came out, it had four to five hundred in a single day, with more than twenty families electing to place their embryos for adoption. The calls weren't restricted to the United States either; one came from as far away as Australia.

One call was from a genetic mother in New York who had eight embryos. Marlene phoned her back, and the woman explained that she and her husband had been praying for an answer as to what to do with the embryos. She said they were her son's brothers and sisters, and she just couldn't destroy them. Then she read the Focus article and said it was an answer to prayer.

This was just the beginning. The day the broadcast aired, "we literally had people sitting there writing down addresses from callers," J. D. said. "'Yes, we'll send out the information.' That was a crazy day for us." The office received more than one thousand inquiries from potential adopting families and nearly one hundred from genetic families interested in placing embryos. So many couples were going through the same anguish we had encountered and were stunned to hear that there was now an option for infertile couples to experience the joy of pregnancy and childbirth. We heard of one woman in Hawaii who, while listening to the radio broadcast in her car, pulled over to the side of the road, overcome with emotion. This was not our doing—that needs to be emphasized and repeated. It was God's doing.

In hindsight, we began to see God's will at work on several levels. Initially we had seen only the myriad pieces that had to fall in place just to finally grow our family with Hannah's blessed arrival. We had only wanted a baby, and once we had one, that might have been the end of it. But it wasn't. Dr. Dobson embraced the concept of embryo adoption and became a vocal advocate of it. This was an enormous boost that allowed thousands of babies—and ultimately will allow tens and even hundreds of thousands—to be rescued from their frozen orphanages.

God was far from done with us and with others who had played a role in our quest to have a baby. What began with Hannah's birth— the culmination of a prolonged, difficult, and emotional journey for Marlene and me—would draw us into a controversy that led all the way to the Oval Office and the Vatican. Our journey was to continue. Our destination: the intersection of faith, family, politics, and science.

CHAPTER 6

The Great Debate

FAITH AND FAMILY have been twin pillars of the American story, but often they've been incompatible with politics and science. In 1996, Dolly the sheep famously (or infamously) was cloned, creating a concern among many in the Christian community and elsewhere that it might be the first step toward attempts to clone a human being. Just because you can doesn't necessarily mean you should.

Science was cooking up another such ethical conflict in a Wisconsin laboratory in the summer of 1998, spearheaded by Dr. James A. Thomson. A brilliant man, Dr. Thomson was a member of the prestigious honor society Phi Beta Kappa while earning a bachelor of science degree in biophysics from the University of Illinois. He went on to earn two doctorate degrees from the University of Pennsylvania, one in veterinary science, the other in molecular biology. He is the director of regenerative biology at the Morgridge Institute for Research in Madison, Wisconsin, as well as a professor of cell and regenerative biology at the University of Wisconsin-Madison. Here is how he is introduced on Morgridge's website:

In 1998, Dr. James Thomson isolated the first human embryonic stem cell, effectively ushering in a new field of scientific research. Undifferentiated cells with remarkable potential, embryonic stem cells can both proliferate without limit and become any of the differentiated cells of the body. As a research tool, human embryonic cells allow unprecedented access to the cellular components of the body, with significant applications in basic research, drug discovery and transplantation medicine.[1]

The remarkable potential to which this refers is the possibility that stem cells extracted from human embryos—created via in vitro fertilization and cryogenically preserved by couples who had completed their families—could be used to help cure many of our most debilitating diseases and injuries. Among these are Parkinson's disease, spinal cord injuries, cancers, diabetes, and Alzheimer's disease.

The scientific breakthrough was revealed in *Science* magazine on November 5, 1998, just eight weeks before Hannah's birth. It was widely heralded, appearing on the front pages of both the *New York Times* and *Washington Post* the following day. The *Times's* headline read, "Scientists Cultivate Cells at Root of Human Life."

Embryonic stem cell research began to accelerate. In its December 17, 1999, special issue, *Science* magazine celebrated the research as its "Breakthrough of the Year."

Late last year, in a technological breakthrough that triggered a burst of research and a whirlwind of ethical debate, two teams of researchers announced that they had managed to prolong the moment of cellular youth. They kept embryonic and fetal human cells at their maximum potential, ready to be steered into becoming any cell in the body.

Building on that achievement, in 1999 developmental biologists and biomedical researchers published more than a dozen landmark papers on the remarkable abilities of these so-called stem cells. We salute this work, which raises hopes of dazzling medical applications and also forces scientists to reconsider fundamental ideas about how cells grow up, as 1999's Breakthrough of the Year.[2]

The ethical debate, as the article noted, began to accelerate as well. In some circles it even was turning vitriolic, most of the vitriol coming from one side (hint: it wasn't the pro-life Christian side), years before Twitter was around to provide a platform for such invective. At issue was the fact that extracting the stem cells destroys the embryos.

On one side of the debate were pro-life Christians and others who recognize that life begins at conception, as well as those who question the morality of using human embryos as instruments for research out of concern about the proverbial slippery slope. They included Pope John Paul II, who in his 1995 encyclical, *Evangelium Vitae*, wrote, "the number of embryos produced is often greater than that needed for implantation in the woman's womb, and these so-called 'spare embryos' are then destroyed or used for research which, under the pretext of scientific or medical progress, in fact reduces human life to the level of simple 'biological material' to be freely disposed of. . . . It must nonetheless be stated that the use of human embryos or fetuses as an object of experimentation constitutes a crime against their dignity as human beings who have a right to the same respect owed to a child once born, just as to every person."[3]

The issue touched us personally, as it did those who were going through the process of adopting frozen embryos and those considering it. Hannah was living proof of what was at stake. She was the result of an embryo having been given a chance—the same chance to which all embryos in frozen storage are entitled. We were angry.

On the other side was everyone else, including a compliant media and a substantially larger and more influential coalition that was universally eager and ready to commit federal funds to embryonic stem cell research.

Among them was prominent syndicated columnist Michael Kinsley, who, on August 29, 2000, wrote a column that appeared in the *Washington Post* and other publications mocking those opposed to embryonic stem cell research on ethical grounds. "Opposition to stem-cell research is the *reductio ad absurdum* [reduction to the absurd] of the right-to-life argument," Kinsley wrote. "A goldfish resembles a human being more than an embryo does." Kinsley also wrote that "the beginning of human life is not a factual question" and that "human life is a label we confer."[4]

The idea that human life is a label we confer was a dangerous precept, as George Weigel, a senior fellow at the Ethics and Public Policy Center in Washington, DC, noted in a column in the *Los Angeles Times*:[5]

> That personhood is a status "we confer" was the argument made in the 1920s by German legal scholar Karl Binding and eminent German psychiatrist Alfred Hoche to promote the notion that the state had an obligation to rid itself of those whose lives were "unworthy of life"—the radically handicapped, for instance. That notion of "life unworthy of life" helped set the cultural ground for the Holocaust.

Weigel further wrote:

> Nothing that is human was ever anything other than human. Nothing that is not human will ever become human. Logic 101 gets us that far. But those logical truths are confirmed by biology and genetics, which make it pluperfectly clear that from the moment of conception, a distinctive, human identity is formed. Absent natural catastrophe or lethal intervention, the distinctive creature formed at the moment of conception will be, indisputably, a human being. It will not be a goldfish or a golden retriever. A human embryo is not merely "capable of life." It is human life. That tiny organism is not, as the New York Times article had it, "a microscopic clump of cells." It is precisely what a human being looks like at that point in its life. It's precisely what Kinsley looked like at that point in his

life. To refuse to acknowledge this is to declare oneself logically impaired, grossly ignorant of genetics and embryology, or both.

Logic is not necessarily a commodity in politics.

There were actually two issues at play, each of them important. First, human embryos should not be used for research purposes, period, though it was legal to do so and was already taking place. Second, taxpayer dollars should not go to fund the research of a process so many found morally objectionable.

To the first point, everyone had been in agreement in the wake of World War II and the medical atrocities committed by German scientists. In 1948, the Declaration of Geneva was adopted by the General Assembly of the World Medical Association. It began, "At the time of being admitted as a member of the medical profession . . ." It was followed by several articles, including this: "I will maintain the utmost respect for human life from the time of conception." The sentence was still in place when the declaration was amended in 1968, but when it was next amended in 1983, "from the time of conception" became "from its beginning."

What had happened in the intervening years? *Roe v. Wade.* When the declaration was amended again in 2005, the sentence had been reduced to "I will maintain the utmost respect for human life." It doesn't take a medical degree to understand why. Abortion is easier to justify without "life begins at conception" throwing up a roadblock.

So is embryonic stem cell research.

It was the latter point, whether to federally fund embryonic stem cell research, that Congress began to consider. In 2000, the United States Senate Committee on Appropriations held three hearings on the matter. Three high-profile celebrities—actors Christopher Reeve, Mary Tyler Moore, and Michael J. Fox—testified on behalf of the government funding embryonic stem cell research. Reeve had become a quadriplegic in a fall from a horse, Moore was a lifelong diabetic, and Fox had been diagnosed with Parkinson's disease. I can say unequivocally that Marlene and I admired all three of them and had watched their movies and television shows. To us they were Superman, the woman who turned the world on with her smile, and Marty McFly and Alex P. Keaton. We, along with tens of millions of Americans, were sympathetic to their plights. All three made compelling witnesses, as did the medical experts recruited to testify.

The side making the ethical argument against federal funding was no match if celebrity were the only metric. Fortunately, it wasn't. Dr. David A. Prentice, like Dr. James A. Thompson, is also a brilliant man, a professor of life sciences at Indiana State at the time, a founding member of Do No Harm: The Coalition of Americans for Research Ethics, an adjunct professor of medical and molecular genetics at the Indiana University School of Medicine, and a science fellow for Senator Sam Brownback (R-Kansas).

Also on board were Pastor Russell Saltzman of Ruskin Heights Lutheran Church in Kansas City, Missouri, and Dr. Micheline M. Mathews-Roth, an associate professor of medicine at Harvard Medical School.

Pastor Saltzman, like Mary Tyler Moore, is a diabetic. He entered an elevator to take him to the second floor of the Hart Senate Office Building, and Moore got in behind him. When they exited, Pastor Saltzman introduced himself, noting that he was testifying for the opposition. But at the behest of his daughter Elizabeth, he asked if he could get Moore's autograph.

"Only if you promise to change your testimony," Moore replied, though cheerily. She then complied, signing, "To Elizabeth with best wishes."

"Above the *i* in wishes, she drew a little heart, just as Mary Richards would have done," Dr. Saltzman wrote in an article on his testimony for the magazine *Touchstone*.[6]

In the first of three hearings, on April 26, 2000, Senator Tom Harkin

(D-Iowa) said this: "I put something on this piece of paper, and I will bet no one out there can tell me what is on that piece of paper because you cannot see it. But I took my pencil and I put a dot on it. That is how big we are talking about. That is how big the human embryo is that we are talking about. In fact, in most cases you cannot even see it with the naked eye."[7]

Senator Arlen Specter (R-Pennsylvania) then introduced Reeve. "We thank you very much, Mr. Reeve, for your personal crusade on stem cells," he said. "We noted with America generally, and the world, the traumatic experience you had with your accident on horseback and the severing of your spinal column, but you have come back to lead this crusade in a very inspirational way. . . . I know that this is a matter of—well, it is of life concern to you. It is that important. Possible regeneration of your spinal column to enable you to fly again. . . . We now turn the floor to you."

Reeve was an impressive witness, as one might expect.

> A critical factor in the quality of life for present and future generations will be what we do with human embryonic stem cells. These cells have the potential to cure disease and conditions ranging from Parkinson's and MS to diabetes, heart disease, to Alzheimer's, Lou Gehrig's, even spinal cord injuries like my own. They have been called the body's self-repair kit.
>
> Their extraordinary potential is a recent discovery. And much basic research needs to be done before they can be sent to the front lines in the battle against diseases. But no obstacle should stand in the way of responsible investigation of their possibilities. To that end, the work should be turned over to the Federal Government through the National Institutes of Health. . . .
>
> In conclusion, I wish to submit a letter of support from four theologians representing the Protestant, Catholic, Jewish, and

Islamic faiths. . . . And finally, I wish to enter into the record a list of over ninety disease groups, clinicians, foundations, universities, and medical schools, all of whom have endorsed my testimony. While we prolong the stem cell debate, millions continue to suffer. It is time to harness the power of government and go forward.

On September 14, 2000, Mary Tyler Moore and Michael J. Fox testified, and Senator Specter introduced them both. He called Moore— accurately, I would add—"the distinguished star of radio, stage, and screen . . . who has been an active advocate for more than a decade, to my personal knowledge, probably best known for her television roles in the *Dick Van Dyke Show* and the *Mary Tyler Moore Show*, received an Emmy in 1992 for her role in *Stolen Babies*, and was nominated for an Oscar in *Ordinary People*. Broadway honored Ms. Moore with a special Tony for *Whose Life Is It Anyway?*"

The irony, no doubt lost on Specter, was that "stolen babies" and "whose life is it anyway?" articulated a position and a question of those who *opposed* using human embryos for research purposes.

"She has lived with diabetes for over thirty years and has worked to raise public and congressional awareness for this disease," Specter said, continuing. "For the last sixteen years she has served as the international chairman of the Juvenile Diabetes Foundation, and last week I saw her leading an entourage on the first floor of the Hart Senate Office Building on her lobbying ways."

Moore, too, gave a compelling testimony, after which Senator Harkin, apparently proud of his pencil dot analogy, brought it up again.

"Mary, I did this once before. I held up a piece of paper. Can you tell me what is on that piece of paper?" he asked.

"You have got to be joking," Moore replied. "No."

"There is teeny little pencil dot that I put on there that you cannot even see," Harkin said. "That is the size of the embryos we are talking

about. I think a lot of people get confused, thinking an embryo is something, almost like a fetus or something like that, fully developed fetus.
We are talking about something less than the size of a pencil dot."

By this time we had become aware that a movement was afoot to use
taxpayers' money to fund embryonic stem cell research. When Marlene
heard what Harkin had said, she was in tears. She understandably took
Harkin's pencil dot analogy personally. A few months later, when I
came home from wherever I'd been, this is how she greeted me:

"Our little dot just put Winnie the Pooh in the toilet today."

Moore, meanwhile, cribbed Michael Kinsley's column in concluding her testimony. "The embryos that are being discussed, according
to science, bear as much resemblance to a human being as a goldfish,"
she said. "I think it makes the answer clear. We are dealing with flesh
and blood people now who feel pain, feel fear, feel debilitation, and our
obligation is to those who are here."

"Very cogently and movingly stated," Specter replied.

Up next was Michael J. Fox, "who has had a spectacular career, first
as Alex P. Keaton on the television series, *Family Ties*, later in a number
of movies, including *Back to the Future*, and most recently on television
again in the highly acclaimed *Spin City*," Specter said. "This past week,
Mr. Fox won an Emmy award for best actor in a comedy series for his
work in *Spin City*. He was diagnosed with Parkinson's in 1991 at the age
of 30, and since announcing his retirement from *Spin City*, he has been
devoting his time to the Michael J. Fox Foundation for Parkinson's
Research."

Fox was a terrific advocate for his position.

It was during a hearing in September 1999 that senators provided exciting testimony as to just how close we may be to a
cure for Parkinson's. In pursuit of that cure, I am back this year
to lend my voice and that of the Michael J. Fox Foundation for
Parkinson's Research to support federal funding for pluripotent

stem cell research. . . . I do not intend to become a professional witness. I am not a politician, nor am I a doctor, nor a research scientist. You do not need me to explain embryonic stem cell research or its medical applications, so what does qualify me to be at this table?

The answer is simple. I am one of a million involuntary experts on Parkinson's disease in the United States battling its destructive nature as we wait for a cure. We need a rescue, and the country should know it.

I wholeheartedly agreed. We needed a rescue for Parkinson's disease and a host of other ailments. That was never an issue. We differed only on how to pursue that rescue, insisting on an ethical approach that wouldn't destroy human embryos. Senator Sam Brownback made this point clear in his prepared statement in these hearings.

"As this subcommittee is well aware, Congress outlawed federal funding for harmful human embryo research in 1996 and has maintained that prohibition ever since," he said. "The ban is broad-based and specific. Funds cannot be used for—and I quote now from the act—'research in which a human embryo or embryos are destroyed, discarded, or knowingly subjected to risk of injury or death.' The intent of Congress is clear. If a research project requires the destruction of human embryos, no federal funds should be used for this project."

Brownback argued that human embryonic stem cell research was not necessary. "And this is a key point, because I want to see people healed, which is what the chairman is after, which is what the ranking member is after. We want to see these diseases [no longer] hit our people or anybody else across the planet. That is our heart and that is our objective, and on that we all agree. That is why I am saying this is not necessary. We can go on the areas of legitimate research into adult stem cells which do not create the moral and ethical difficulties that we do in human embryo stem cell research."

Dr. Mathews-Roth, meanwhile, made it a point to note that she was not there representing Harvard Medical School, though having Harvard Medical School on a resume did lend gravitas to her position on this matter.

"The embryological fact is that we do know when a new life begins, and that is at fertilization, when egg and sperm join," she said.

> Now, stem cells are not embryos, but as Dr. Prentice was pointing out, the human ones seem to be a little bit more totipotent than mouse embryo cells, but remember, you have to break apart an embryo to get the stem cells, and this is really the ethical objection. So I think we all have to ask ourselves, do we really want to allow the deliberate killing of even one of the youngest members of our species to help sick members of our own species also?
>
> It is a tough ethical question, but again, can we really do this, because we know ethically that a good end can never justify using a bad means, or an evil means to attain it?

There was a great deal more from both sides, but here we'll give the last words to Senator Specter and Dr. Prentice. This is their exchange on what to do with frozen embryos should genetic parents not intend to use them and if they would not be used for research:

Dr. Prentice: Senator, I am not sure that, from my own perspective, I could justify even discarding those embryos.

Senator Specter: You cannot justify what, sir?

Dr. Prentice: Discarding the embryos . . . so what do we do with all of those embryos[?] . . . Perhaps that is something that Congress itself should be looking at in terms of the IVF industry.

Senator Specter: Well, what would the alternative be?

Dr. Prentice: I am not certain, sir, until we can get them adopted, or what the answer might be.

Senator Specter: Well, they have to be carried to term. Are you suggesting that the government would compel someone, a woman to carry them to term?

Dr. Prentice: I do not think we should be in the business of compelling anyone to carry these embryos to term or destroy them, either way.

Senator Specter: Well then, what would you do?

Dr. Prentice: I think it would have to be perhaps some sort of an adoption program, but that is not really the focus of the issue.

Senator Specter: I agree with you, but you brought it up, so I wanted to explore it if you care to. What would you do with them, if not discard them? If there were another alternative to discarding them, I think you have a very valid point.

Dr. Prentice: I have not really thought through the issue, Senator, but as we mentioned, one possibility might be some sort of adoption program.

Senator Specter: How would you structure an adoption program?

Dr. Prentice: I am not really certain. I have not really had time to think through the issue. It has really just come up.

We already knew how an adoption program would be structured, how one already had been structured. Dr. Prentice and Marlene soon became acquaintances and allies as the debate carried into 2001 and the first year of George W. Bush's presidency.

CHAPTER 7

Hannah Goes to Washington

WE WOULD EVENTUALLY join the official fray over embryonic stem cell research in 2001. But we had already begun supporting the movement against federal funding of embryonic stem cell research in 2000.

When Human Life Advocates Inc., the advocacy affiliate of the Christian Legal Society's Center for Law and Religious Freedom, asked us to be plaintiffs in a lawsuit, we agreed. The lawsuit, to be brought against the National Institutes of Health and Donna Shalala, secretary of Health and Human Services, challenged the NIH's new Guidelines on Human Pluripotent Stem Cell Research that violated the 1996 Dickey-Wicker Amendment. This amendment, passed by Congress and signed by President Clinton, banned federal funding for research on embryos. But the ban had occurred before Dr. James Thomson had made his discovery, isolating the first human embryonic stem cell that opened an avenue of research that destroys the embryos.

The NIH attempted an end run around the Dickey-Wicker Amendment by issuing guidelines stating that, while obtaining embryonic stem cells had to be privately funded, federal funds could be used for research on them once they were obtained. The Clinton administration agreed.

Say this for convictions in Washington: they're malleable.

We had been told that the lawsuit was unlikely to go to trial, and it did not. The legal challenge in which we were to participate was absorbed by a similar lawsuit filed in the US District Court for the District of Columbia on March 8, 2001. It was brought by our adoption agency,

Nightlight Christian Adoptions, as part of a coalition that included the Christian Medical Association and others. The suit was filed against the NIH and Tommy Thompson, who had been appointed only a month earlier by the newly inaugurated President George W. Bush as his secretary of Health and Human Services. Secretary Thompson, incidentally, had expressed concern over the guidelines and had already begun an independent legal review.

"The suit had the effect of creating a moratorium on the federal funding of embryonic stem cell research," the *Embryo Project Encyclopedia* notes. "The Honorable Royce C. Lambert issued a stay order on 4 May 2001, suspending the case while the Bush administration reviewed the NIH guidelines."[1]

Throughout this process, Marlene had begun frequent correspondence with Samuel B. Casey, a Christian attorney prominent for his relentless defense of the sanctity of human life and notably active on behalf of ethical stem cell research that did not include the destruction of human embryos. He quickly recognized that Marlene's passion on this subject matched his own, as did her eloquence in defending the pro-life position. When the House of Representatives scheduled a subcommittee hearing in advance of President Bush making a decision on federal funding of embryonic stem cell research, Casey implored Marlene to testify. He noted that politics involves real-life stories, that it's difficult to attract political attention without putting a human face to the issue. Hannah was that human face.

Marlene initially was hesitant only because, beyond friends and family, we had not revealed Hannah's story except with pseudonyms. She told Mr. Casey that should she agree to testify, she preferred not to do so alone, and in the meantime, she would pray about it.

We can't say unequivocally that a VeggieTales video influenced her decision, but neither can we say it didn't. Hannah had been introduced to the Christian cartoon series, and we quickly developed a library of VeggieTales videos. One of them was *Esther, the Girl Who Became*

Queen, a story based on the book of Esther in the Bible. Marlene was watching it with Hannah one day. In the story, Esther wondered why she had become queen, and her cousin, Mordecai, told her God had put her in that position for a reason. Mordecai sang, in rhyme, that we need not fear anything, that God would guide us and guard us.

Cartoon or not, those words were timely and biblical, and they found an attentive target in Marlene, who jotted them down. She called Dr. Dobson to get his opinion on whether she should testify to the subcommittee. At the end of their conversation, he said what she needed to hear, echoing the story of Esther: "Marlene, it appears the Lord has prepared you for such a time as this. I have two words for you: do it!"

We did not seek this fight, but neither was it one in which we were willing to cede responsibility to others. We are pro-life Christians who believe life begins at conception, and unwittingly, we were at the fore of an embryo adoption movement that began to allow countless other embryos in frozen storage to be given the same opportunities that Hannah had. We were obligated to make a stand on behalf of those who cannot speak for themselves, as the Bible instructs us to do, and we agreed to do so.

Marlene reluctantly but prayerfully agreed to testify, understanding that the cause was greater than her concerns. "We agreed [to testify]," her notes from that period said. "Very stressful. Lost 9# in 3 wks. . . . Many conversations with God (*Do you know what you are asking me to do? I just wanted a baby*)."

Marlene, the mother of Hannah, the first Snowflake baby, would testify. She successfully recruited Lucinda Borden, the mother of the second and third Snowflake babies, twins Mark and Luke, to testify as well. Friend JoAnn Davidson, the director of the Snowflakes Embryo Adoption Program at Nightlight Christian Adoptions, also was asked to testify.

We knew what we were facing by venturing into the cauldron of politics on the front lines in Washington, DC, with a pro-life position with which many would disagree—even some whom we have always held in the highest regard. Among them was renowned *Washington Post* columnist Charles Krauthammer.

"As the Bush administration approaches a decision on stem cell research, the caricatures have already been drawn," he wrote in his column published on June 29, 2001. "On one side are the human benefactors who wish only a chance to use the remarkable potential of stem cells—primitive cells that have the potential to develop into any body tissue with the proper tweaking—to cure a myriad of diseases. On the other side stand the Catholic Church and the usual anti-abortion zealots who, because of squeamishness about the fate of a few clumps of cells, will prevent this great boon to humanity."[2]

When the word *zealot* is used, it usually is done so pejoratively, as was the word *caricature* in this instance. Our admiration for Krauthammer notwithstanding, this particular column was a disappointment. One headline to his column at least sounded a note of reservation ("Pursue stem cell research, but with caution"), as did the first and second paragraphs. But his wording committed a deceptive omission: neither we nor anyone else involved in embryo adoption have ever had any objections to stem cell research per se. Rather, we have openly encouraged adult stem cell research. Our opposition was specific to embryonic stem cell research that would destroy embryos. Krauthammer's failure to make that distinction would, unfortunately, become a staple of mainstream media reports, whether by ignorance or by design. Either way, it was unacceptable.

Krauthammer's cautionary note was nevertheless forceful:

> I happen to favor federal support for stem cell research, but unless we treat the opposition arguments with respect, rather than reflexive disdain, we will fail to appreciate the looming dangers—moral and biological—inherent in this unprecedentedly powerful new technique. . . .
>
> It is important to recognize the gravity of providing

government money—and thus communal moral sanction—to the deliberate destruction of a human embryo for the purpose of research. It violates the categorical imperative that human life be treated as an end and not a means.

It is a serious objection and should be set aside only with great trepidation.[3]

❄

The hearing was scheduled for July 17 at 2:05 p.m. in room 2154 of the Rayburn House Office Building on Independence Avenue, across the street from the US Capitol. We weren't sure what to expect by way of media coverage; we assumed the hearing would receive some, but with all that was going on in Washington in the first months of President George W. Bush's presidency, we thought coverage might be minimal. I hoped so, at least. I had never spoken of our story to any of my coworkers, not from any sense of guilt or embarrassment but strictly for privacy reasons; we thought it sufficient that our families and friends were aware of it. Hannah was our daughter, and that was the end of it.

My news judgment in this instance failed me. When we entered the hearing chamber, it immediately was apparent that this hearing was not going to escape notice. It was standing room only and included a dozen or more photographers. Senator Orrin Hatch (R-Utah) was among those in attendance, though this was a House of Representatives hearing.

Each side was well represented, though who was on which side was not immediately apparent. For instance, among those testifying was a sixteen-year-old leukemia patient, a wonderful young man, whose malady would have suggested he favored embryonic stem cell research. But though struggling with serious health concerns, he was a Christian guided by his faith and was steadfastly against destroying embryos for research purposes.

Then there was Dr. C. Christopher Hook, a hematologist and internist from the prestigious Mayo Clinic in Rochester, Minnesota. His resume suggested he might be another voice on behalf of the research. But that assumption, too, was wrong. Dr. Hook was a senior fellow of the Center for Bioethics and Human Dignity and a member of the Christian Medical Association's Ethics Commission.

The hearing room itself was no different than what we expected. The politicians were seated on an elaborate dais in front of a table with microphones for those testifying. Directly behind the table was a row of chairs for those waiting to testify and their families. Behind that row, several more rows of chairs were provided for other attendees, including the news media. The photographers were on either side of the room and on the ground beneath the dais.

It was daunting to see familiar Republicans and Democrats on the dais. Here's how the official record from the opening of the hearings read:

> The subcommittee met, pursuant to notice, at 2:05 p.m., in room 2154, Rayburn House Office Building, Hon. Mark E. Souder (chairman of the subcommittee) presiding.
>
> Present: Representatives Souder, Gilman, Mica, Ose, Jo Ann Davis of Virginia, Weldon, Cummings, Blagojevich, Allen, and Schakowsky.
>
> Also present: Senator Hatch, and Representatives Burton, Lewis of Kentucky, Smith of New Jersey, Waxman, and Maloney.[4]

We were already familiar with Representatives Souder and Chris Smith for their staunch support of pro-life issues. Obviously we knew of Senator Hatch, and Democratic Rep. Henry Waxman was known to us because he was from the west side of Los Angeles.

The hearing was presided over by Congressman Souder (R-Indiana), who endeared himself to us forever with his opening remarks. "Before we begin," he said, "I would like to thank three people in this room who are here on behalf of thousands of other children in this country. Hannah, Luke, and Mark are too young to understand their impact on the debate currently before this body, but their presence is truly a reminder that every child, every life is precious."

Congressman Elijah Cummings (D-Maryland) began the proceedings, and his remarks included this: "Whether or not the Federal Government funds research using embryonic stem cells, that research is certain to proceed in the private sector. As William Safire put it in a recent *New York Times* op-ed, 'The stem cell genie is out of the research bottle. Whether driven by private funds here or by the investment of money by foreign governments,' Safire writes, 'embryonic cells will be used to achieve breakthroughs to cures.'"

Safire was a former speechwriter for President Richard Nixon and a self-described libertarian conservative who was coming down on the same side as probably most others from the most influential liberal voice in America, the *New York Times*.

Up next was Senator Hatch. We had assumed that a pro-life senator would come down, well, on the pro-life side. But from our viewpoint, he turned out to be a hostile witness.

> Let me make clear at the outset that I consider myself to be strongly pro-life. I am vigorously opposed to abortion, and I always have been and always will be. The theme of your hearing today is that there are alternatives to embryonic stem cell research such as adult stem cell research or adoption of embryos. The lovely children and their families who have traveled here today prove that there can be good alternatives. By all means, let these good alternatives proceed.
>
> But I also think we would be making a critical mistake if we were to shut off the avenue of research that scientists have found to be the most promising at this point, embryonic stem cell research. Over the past months I have devoted countless

hours of study to this important issue, reflecting on my spiritual teachings, the law, the science, and the ethical issues presented by embryonic stem cell research. My conclusion was that the support of embryonic stem cell research is consistent with pro-life and pro-family values. This research holds out promise for improving and extending life for more than one hundred million Americans suffering from a variety of diseases, including heart disease, Parkinson's, Alzheimer's, ALS, multiple sclerosis, cancer, and diabetes.

Senator Hatch never looked at us and, in fact, when he had finished, he stood up and left without hearing any further testimony. This was exceedingly disappointing that a leading pro-life senator could not acknowledge the simple fact that life begins at conception, thus passing on an opportunity to make a stand on behalf of those who cannot speak for themselves.

The last politician to give an opening statement was Congressman Smith (R-New Jersey), one of the leading pro-life politicians in Washington, DC. He brought gravitas to the debate, speaking passionately and emphatically on behalf of those whom Hatch had betrayed.

Yesterday I met three wonderful children, Hannah, Mark, and Luke, along with their courageous and loving parents. Hannah, Mark, and Luke are here today to witness to the Congress, the President, and to the world, that every human being, no matter how small, has innate value, dignity, and purpose. They are here today as survivors, having overcome the perils of cryogenic freezing at a very young age. All three have emerged from their frozen orphanages to be loved and cared for by their adoptive parents. They are pioneers, the start of a new chapter in adoption.

And they are, indeed, the lucky ones, because if the President and the Congress decide to federally fund human embryonic stem cell research, which is always fatal to the newly created human being—Mr. [Henry] Waxman earlier mentioned that we just want to study them. To study them, you have to kill them. If we follow that and we federally fund that, a generation of Hannahs, Marks, and Lukes will be lost forever.

These littlest of human beings aren't potential life, but life with vast potential. So I find it highly offensive, insensitive, and inhumane to label human embryos as excess or throw-aways or spare or expendable. Hannah, Mark, and Luke weren't spare; they weren't expendable; they weren't junk. These little kids, like little kids everywhere, are not excess. The miracle of human life deserves more respect than that. Hannah, Mark, and Luke are living proof that tens of thousands of human beings existing today in frozen orphanages can and should be placed with caring adoptive parents, not abandoned as fodder to a person in a white coat demanding more material.

Frozen embryos "aren't potential life, but life with vast potential." If we'd been permitted to applaud, we'd have stood and done so.

Finally, it was time for the witnesses, who were asked to come forward and were sworn in under oath. Their instructions were to push the button on the microphone stand when it was their turn to speak. Marlene was first up; I sat directly behind her, holding two-year-old Hannah, who, with a pacifier in her mouth, eventually fell asleep on my shoulder. Marlene understandably had been exceedingly nervous all morning and early afternoon, unable to eat, and almost visibly shaking—until she pushed the button. At that moment, she said, a veil of complete calm washed over her from head to toe. The only explanation is that our prayers were answered.

She began by laying out our story leading to the first transfer of embryos. She was building to a crescendo, trumpeting truth infused with passion, that from the moment an embryo was conceived it was life that required only the same elements and opportunity that all of us were accorded. It was undeniable and objectionable only to those who did not care about the truth.

During my first transfer, no children successfully implanted. Accordingly, physicians thawed the remaining eight embryos on April [10], 1998. Three survived, including Hannah. The embryologist snapped a picture of Hannah and her siblings for our baby book. No mere dot, she contained the entire blueprint for human life.

Hannah continued to develop overnight outside my body. The physician referred to this as compaction, a process where the cells start to move to one side and a fluid-filled sac began forming. We have a picture of Hannah when this occurred outside my body on April 11, 1998, the day she and her siblings were transferred into my uterus.

On April 20, 1998, I learned I was pregnant, and an ultrasound on May 4, 1998, confirmed I was pregnant with one baby. Hannah, now safely in my womb, was only receiving from me oxygen, nutrients, a warm place to grow, and love throughout my entire pregnancy. Subsequent ultrasounds showed Hannah was doing just fine.

Hannah Eileen Strege was born on December 31, 1998. She is the best gift parents could have and no different than all children, all of whom were once embryos either in the petri dish or the fallopian tubes.

John and I adopted Hannah long before we knew about public controversy involving embryo stem cell research. Mary Tyler Moore and Senator Tom Harkin sparked our desire to speak out on this issue. We've had to watch Ms. Moore compare our daughter to a goldfish, and Senator Harkin likened her to a dot on a piece of paper and referred to her as expendable. Obviously, she is none of these.

Notwithstanding the message conveyed by the media, John and I care deeply about identifying therapies and cures for serious diseases. As an occupational therapist, I care for many people who have severe disabilities. My mother died from pancreatic cancer. We paid to save our daughter's cord blood at birth to advance umbilical stem cell research designed to overcome serious disease.

Another myth propagated by the media is that embryos exist "in excess of need."

More infertile couples exist than embryos likely to survive thawing. My OB/GYN told me any woman can carry any embryo. Tissue and blood matching is not necessary. As embryo adoption proliferates in the wake of this controversy, the excess supply of embryos will evaporate.

Hannah is an ambassador for the roughly 188,000 frozen human embryos like her in frozen orphanages who could be adopted rather than terminated with assistance from my federal tax dollars. We plead with Congress not to force millions of Americans like me to violate our consciences and participate in another form of genocide, especially when the advances possible with the other stem cells are not nearly exhausted.

In closing, I am very proud to be part of this new generation of adopting mothers.

Pride does not begin to explain how I felt at that moment. Marlene has made a career devoted to helping those in need, and here on a national stage, she had made an important stand on behalf of those who needed only an opportunity.

Lucinda Borden followed with her testimony, while her husband, John, held the two young twins, Luke and Mark. When she was concluding, she introduced her husband, who stood holding the boys, one in each arm.

"I would like to ask every member of this committee, especially the members that aren't here, and that question is: Which one of my children would you kill?" John asked. "Which one would you choose to take? Would you want to take Luke, the giggler, who we call Turbo, or do you want to take the big guy, Tank? Which one would you take?"

It was a mic-drop moment, perfectly delivered.

Lucinda said later, "There was silence after that, and I realized that his impromptu move made all the difference in the world." It also evoked a dark side of humankind, as stands on principles often do. "When we returned home, there were lots of messages from people who hated what we were doing, so we stopped answering the phone."

When Marlene and Lucinda were done testifying, Congressman David Weldon (R-Florida), who also is a physician, had a few questions.

"This was, I think, a pretty revealing thing for you to do, to come all the way to Washington and tell your personal story, as you have, in front of the TV cameras," he said. "I would assume neither of you have ever done anything of this sort before. Could you just comment on what motivated you to agree to come and testify in this kind of an environment and get yourself and your family involved in a debate like this?"

"I guess for me, I've seen these debates on C-SPAN at home, and no one is talking about infertility as a valid diagnosis," Marlene replied. "This is what needs to happen here. These embryos need to be adopted, and I just wanted Americans to know that this is an option, because the media has been saying, well, they're just going to be destroyed anyway, that type of thing. Also, we wanted to come here and meet with the President, too, so he could see our children and see that these are real people, these children."

"Are you scheduled to meet with the President?" Weldon asked.

"Well, we're here. We haven't had anything set up so far. So, do you have any connections?" Marlene asked, eliciting laughter.

"Well, I have been trying to get an appointment myself, and I haven't been able to get one. So, I guess, get in line," he replied. "Hannah is, I would assume, too young to have a comment at all? Does she understand any of this?"

"Did you want to say anything, Hannah?" Marlene replied. Hannah didn't. "I can tell you, though," Marlene said, "that for the last couple of nights we've been really kind of busy, and so I asked her, 'What do you want to pray for tonight?' And two nights in a row she said, 'For the Snowflakes, amen.' So I guess that would be her comment."

Congressman Weldon continued. "How do you feel, because many people, even pro-life people, approach me and say, 'Well, these frozen embryos just aren't children.' Yet, in your testimony, Mrs. Strege, you talk about—we heard one distinguished member here today say that life can't be conceived in a petri dish, and that wasn't really life. Could you elaborate on that a little bit and where you think your children began and how, and watched them evolve?"

"Right," Marlene said. "I have pictures of my daughter over there." She was pointing to a visual display that showed a photo of the embryos when they were removed from frozen storage. "That was the day that she was thawed. The next picture is the next day, the day they transferred her into me. A physician told me that she had gone on to her next stage of human development—that was outside of my body, called compaction, when those cells start to move to one side and a fluid-filled sac starts to form.

"Furthermore, I'm the adoptive mom. The only thing I added to my daughter was oxygen, nutrients, a warm place to grow, and love. That's a scientific fact. So, I mean, you're going to have to tell me what I added to her to be a human life. She went into me as a human life, as an embryo. She came out of me as a human life, as an infant. She is now in her human developmental stage of toddlerhood. I mean, you tell me what I added to her to make her a human life?"

Rep. Jo Ann Davis (R-Virginia) followed up with a question. "The pharmaceutical companies and many scientists would like free rein and taxpayer funding to destroy embryos for research," she said. "What would you say to the pharmaceutical lobbyists who have been demanding Federal funding on embryo destructive research? If they were to come into your offices—and they come into ours—what would you say to them?"

"I would say to look at my daughter and tell me why she's expendable."

The inestimable JoAnn Davidson, director of the Snowflakes Embryo Adoption Program, was called to give her statement, and it was brilliant. I call her inestimable, but Ron Stoddart, speaking as the director of Nightlight Christian Adoptions, went one better.

"J. D. was a godsend," Ron said. "She had the passion and she was articulate. She was a great spokesperson."

Four years earlier, she had been asked to start the embryo adoption program, with no knowledge of the issue and no training that might have assisted her. Yet she became an expert and a gifted, passionate advocate on behalf of embryo adoption who bristled at the characterization of the embryos as tissue or worse. "For me it was always a pro-life battle," she said years later. "This was always letting people know this was a baby waiting to be born rather than a nondescript medical term, *embryo*. Sometimes that made it exhausting. I remember [that] any time I was doing media, and even that testimony, [I was] testifying that these were children and not tissue. This is going to grow up to be a human. It doesn't transport in time from another entity like a monkey or dog. It's a human embryo. When we went to testify, sitting in that room were people curled up with rheumatoid arthritis. They were sitting there saying we want cures for [our] family. I said I want cures for your family. Killing a child isn't a goal. But saying this isn't a child makes you feel like now we can destroy it. Even the words matter."

Her words were powerful and informed that day in Room 2154 of the Rayburn House Office Building.

I am here to let you know today that embryo adoption is not a theory and it's not an idea and it's not a hope, but it is happening right now in America. In fact, all fifty states permit living human embryo adoption and implantation. In fact, embryo adoption is proof positive that all embryos are not destroyed.

There are some who would say that they are going to be destroyed anyway. I'm here to tell you that's not necessary. We in America are greater than that. We can and ought to save every embryo. We can do this through educating the public about embryo adoption. We can do this by way of our IVF clinics including the adoption option in their consent procedures, then to enforce and encourage limitations on the numbers of embryos that are created.

Human embryo adoption is not about "dots on a paper," as Senator Harkin has referred to living human embryos. Rather, this debate is about whether we as an entire society want to federally fund destructive human experimentation of the littlest humans.

Here in this room and in homes across America we must decide whether we should compel every taxpayer to support destroying human embryos at a stage of development through which each one of us has passed. Are we going to accept the effect of genocide as medical therapy? Having looked into the eyes of eight precious newborns and frozen embryos, I, for one, will not.

During the questioning that followed, Rep. Jan Schakowsky (D-Illinois) made the mistake of running afoul of J. D. by characterizing Hannah, Luke, and Mark as "the result of wonderful scientific research." When the congresswoman was finished, J. D. politely asked, "May we respond?"

"Yes, go ahead," Congressman Weldon replied.

"Because I would definitely disagree," J. D. said, and continued:

> These children are not a product of some wonderful medical research. They're a product of the fact that a huge problem exists, that too many embryos have been created. These children were not created as wonderful new research. They were created as live children. This [embryo adoption] program does not exist to provide opportunities for new families to have children. This program exists to solve a problem that exists, and that's 188,000—conservative number—188,000—embryos that are in storage. I think there's a problem that we have that many children existing in clinics. This program is not here to provide a new way for families to get children. It's here to eliminate a problem that currently exists, in that there are children waiting to be born. It's no different than an orphanage, an orphanage that has never been really looked at as a really neat opportunity for somebody to add children to their families. It's been seen as a travesty that these children are not being parented.

Again, had it not been frowned upon, we would have applauded.

Dr. Hook was among the last to testify. Noting in his opening statement that he was there "speaking as a private citizen," not as a representative of the Mayo Foundation, he began with four questions:

> Number one, as a society, are we willing to devalue and commodify members of our human family?
>
> Number two, are we willing to violate principles of human subjects research that have arisen from the ashes of atrocities committed here and abroad under circumstances when other members of the human community have been devalued and commodified for utilitarian logic, precisely as is occurring now in the stem cell debate?

Number three, are we willing to transform our concept of proxy-informed consent for medical care into a license to kill by allowing genetic parents to effectively abandon the offspring they deliberately conceived to fatal medical experimentation under a pretense of informed consent?

Number four, are we willing to set the precedent that the promise, not proof, of future medical treatments for third party patients is sufficient to endorse the destruction of living human beings now?

If it wasn't already clear where he stood, it soon would be with these remarks that followed.

During the Nuremberg war crime trials, conducted at the conclusion of World War II, the German researchers tried for their crimes defended themselves by forwarding this argument: First, there allegedly existed a great need for research in order to save the lives of soldiers and sailors. Two, the subjects of the experiments were already targeted to die. Someone else had made the decision that they were to die; we didn't. And, therefore, three, we should not let this valuable commodity, this chance to learn in ways we otherwise could not, go to waste.

This argument, resoundingly rejected by the Nuremberg tribunal, is precisely the same argument that is being put forward today to justify using government funds and authorizations for research on human embryos. The only difference is that we have substituted human embryos as the group of devalued, commodified human beings who are to be sacrificed on the altar of scientific progress.

Well said.

❊

It had been a stressful and exhausting day, after which we returned to the hotel and ordered room service. We were flying home the following morning, and when we got to the airport, we bought a copy of the *New York Times*. So much for going incognito. The hearing was the lead story in the newspaper, the headline reading, "Stem Cell Debate in House Has Two Faces, Both Young." The story jumped to page 16, where there was a photograph of me holding Hannah, a pacifier in her mouth, sleeping on my shoulder.

Sheryl Gay Stolberg's *Times* story was fair, covering both sides, which was all we could ask. Most of the news coverage, in fact, was balanced, perhaps evocative of a time gone by, when news pages were largely devoid of opinion. Or maybe it was simply considered bad form to criticize parents testifying with their toddlers on hand. "Kind of hard to attack a guy who's holding his baby daughter," Ron Stoddart said.

On the opinion side, two columns stood out, one written a few days before the hearing by Steve Chapman of the *Chicago Tribune*, the other written after the hearing by an Ivy League student in her college newspaper. The student newspaper called us hypocrites, saying that because Hannah was the only embryo of the twenty to survive the thaw and implantation, we had destroyed nineteen of them in our pursuit of one human life. The article said that had we had a successful pregnancy with the first embryo, the others would have remained frozen, while also concluding that nineteen potential lives were destroyed in the process and asking whether we were selfish or compassionate.

Where to begin? The nineteen other embryos were not "destroyed"; they were given a chance, the same as Hannah. This is not what would have happened had they been destroyed for the sake of research. The writer's claim that, had we had a successful pregnancy from the first frozen embryo, the others would have remained frozen is accurate only to the extent that they would have remained frozen until we went for a second pregnancy. Incidentally, had the three embryos all survived the transfer, we'd have joyously welcomed triplets into our family. Our pursuit was not one single human life.

It would be interesting if the writer were able to meet Hannah, now an adult, and ask her whether Marlene and I had been selfish. I don't wish to presume the writer was not a Christian. I'll just note JoAnn Davidson's conclusion on embryo adoption vis-à-vis embryonic stem cell research. "We're actually thawing them in the best protocol we can," she said, "allowing God to be ordaining of their future rather than no option."

Steve Chapman's take, meanwhile, was a professional one. We've never met him nor talked to him. I have not read enough of him through the years to know what his politics are. But on this issue, he got it, and I emailed him to let him know how much we appreciated it. His column said:

> Hannah Strege is 2 years old, blonde-haired and chubby-cheeked. This week, she'll make an appearance in Washington, D.C., so lawmakers can see one alternative to destroying human embryos to advance stem cell research.
>
> Hannah, who once was a frozen embryo, might have been fatally dissected for scientific purposes, but she was lucky enough to escape that fate. Instead, she was allowed to enter this world as the adoptive daughter of John and Marlene Strege, who couldn't conceive on their own. Accompanying the Streges to Capitol Hill will be John and Lucinda Borden, along with their twin 9-month-olds, Mark and Luke.
>
> Paralysis victim Christopher Reeve has testified in favor of federal funding for stem cell research using embryos left over from in vitro fertilizations—an issue now confronting President Bush. Reeve, like his allies, argues that it's unethical to let perfectly good embryos "be tossed away as so much garbage when they could help save thousands of lives."

But the trash can is not the only place they can end up—as these parents, and others, can confirm. If you see these children on the news, ask yourself: Which one would you have chosen to die for science?[5]

Chapman went on to note that Senator Connie Mack (R-Florida) is anti-abortion yet in favor of federal funding for embryonic stem cell research.

"He supports this research because it may yield benefits in the fight against disease. He may be right, but the progress won't come free. If Mack wants to see the cost of such efforts, he might take time this week to say hello to Hannah Strege."[6]

Even reading this column today, eighteen years later, gives me goosebumps.

❄

On July 23, 2001, President Bush met with Pope John Paul II at his summer residence at Castel Gandolfo outside Rome, and the pope came down strongly on the pro-life, anti-embryonic stem cell research side.

"Another area in which political and moral choices have the gravest consequences for the future of civilization concerns the most fundamental of human rights, the right to life itself," the pope said. "Experience is already showing how a tragic coarsening of consciences accompanies the assault on innocent human life in the womb, leading to accommodation and acquiescence in the face of other related evils, such as euthanasia, infanticide, and most recently, proposals for the creation for research purposes of human embryos, destined to destruction in the process.

"A free and virtuous society, which America aspires to be, must reject practices that devalue and violate human life at any stage from conception to natural death."[7]

Later that day in a joint news conference with Italian prime minister Silvio Berlusconi, President Bush responded to the pope's strong stand.

"I'll take that point of view into consideration as I make up my mind on a very difficult issue confronting the United States of America," he said. "I do care about the opinions of people, particularly someone as profound as the Holy Father."[8]

Now we went into waiting mode.

CHAPTER 8

President Bush Makes the Call

WHEN YOU ARE a sportswriter—or married to one—vacations often are folded into business trips. One of them occurred for us in August of 2001, when I was going to Colorado for the International presented by Qwest, a PGA Tour event in Castle Pines, south of Denver. Marlene and Hannah came along so they could visit friends in Colorado Springs while I worked. This, of course, included the obligatory trip to Focus on the Family so that Hannah could play in the Kids' Korner in the Welcome Center and my wife could renew friendships.

Marlene, with Hannah in tow, dropped me at Castle Pines Golf Club, then drove down to Colorado Springs. After they had arrived at Focus on the Family, word got upstairs to Dr. Dobson that they were there, and he invited them up to his office. He was interested in hearing how Marlene's testimony in the congressional hearing had gone. He then asked her to go down to the radio studio to tell her story about going to Washington. These types of interviews are recorded and then edited to fit time slots, and only later would it be determined when it would air across the Focus on the Family radio network.

Dr. Dobson began by setting up the issue. "This subject has become a matter of great controversy recently," he said. "That is why I wanted you to come down to tell us about it today. President Bush, even as we speak, apparently is trying to decide whether to allocate the use of federal money to kill those embryos and make use of the stem cells for research purposes."[1]

He noted that Marlene had called him for advice on whether she should go to Washington and put herself through all that. "I know it was a very stressful thing to do, but you agreed to do it. I think I told you, you need to let the Lord make use of this."

"It is really his story, what happened to us," she replied. "We could see how God orchestrated this whole thing with our getting our daughter and that I was able to give birth to her. It was stressful. [Also] on our panel were another Snowflake mother, who gave birth to twins who are ten months old, and the director of the Snowflake program. I think the three of us held our own."

"You sure did," Dr. Dobson said. "Your picture and Hannah's picture have been in newspapers all across the country. You've had tremendous publicity from that, and the Lord used that to say those are babies out there. They're not just meaningless protoplasm, they're not goldfish, they're not dots on a page. This is life."

Near the end of their discussion, Dr. Dobson called for Hannah.

"Okay, Hannah, we've talked to your mom. Come on over here and sit on my lap. I'm so glad to see you. Do you pray to Jesus?"

"Yeah," Hannah replied.

"Does he tell you he loves you? You know he loves you, don't you?"

"Yeah."

Marlene asked her who she prays for.

"The Snowflakes," Hannah said.

Then Dr. Dobson asked her if she'd sing a song for him.

She began singing, the words unmistakable even from her sweet, though not fully developed, two-and-a-half-year-old voice:

Jesus loves the little children
All the children of the world,
Red and yellow, black and white
All are precious in his sight
Jesus loves the little children of the world.

"Wasn't that special?" Dr. Dobson said, audibly moved. "What a beautiful little girl she is."

This conversation, recorded on August 1, became part of a longer broadcast on human cloning and stem cell research. It was sent out via satellite to Focus's radio accounts on Wednesday, August 8, for airing on Thursday, August 9.

Meanwhile, President Bush's impending decision on whether to permit federal funding for embryonic stem cell research was not expected for a few weeks, maybe by Labor Day weekend. Yet that same Thursday morning, word came that President Bush had made a decision that he would announce in a nationally televised address from his ranch in Crawford, Texas, that evening.

Dr. Dobson had the uneasy feeling that the president was preparing to make "the wrong decision," noting that "the signals coming out of the White House on Thursday afternoon were that this was going the wrong way." That afternoon, Dr. Dobson invited all thirteen hundred staff at Focus on the Family to gather for "an intense season of prayer."

"There were tears during that time," he said. "There were many prayers. At one point all of us were on our knees asking the Lord to talk to the president and communicate to him and to protect those precious babies and those lives, asking the Lord not to let this great country to fall down this slippery slope."

The segment with Hannah singing "Jesus Loves the Little Children" was played, after which everyone there joined together in singing the song. When we heard about this later, we were humbled that our desire to have a baby had eventually contributed to so noble a cause.

Finally the time arrived, and President Bush delivered his conclusion to the nation. He began by laying out both sides of the issue. He noted the advances already made and that "scientists believe further research using stem cells offers great promise that could help improve the lives of those who suffer from many terrible diseases, from juvenile diabetes to Alzheimer's, from Parkinson's to spinal cord injuries. And while scientists admit they are not yet certain, they believe stem cells derived from embryos have unique potential."[2]

He also highlighted the often overlooked fact that stem cells from sources other than embryos—"from adult cells, from umbilical cords that are discarded after babies are born, from human placentas"—also are promising and are already helping with treatments on "patients suffering from a range of diseases." He even pointed out that scientists believed embryonic stem cells held the greatest potential for cures, but that without federal funds, progress would be slow and "the best and brightest scientists" would be reluctant to participate.

Then the president got to the "profound ethical questions":

> Extracting the stem cell destroys the embryo, and thus destroys its potential for life. Like a snowflake, each of these embryos is unique, with the unique genetic potential of an individual human being.
>
> As I thought through this issue, I kept returning to two fundamental questions. First, are these frozen embryos human life and therefore something precious to be protected? And second, if they're going to be destroyed anyway, shouldn't they be used for a greater good, for research that has the potential to save and improve other lives? . . .
>
> On the first issue, are these embryos human life? Well, one researcher told me he believes this five-day-old cluster of cells is not an embryo, not yet an individual, but a pre-embryo. He argued that it has the potential for life, but it is not a life because it cannot develop on its own. An ethicist dismissed that as a callous attempt at rationalization. "Make no mistake," he told me, "that cluster of cells is the same way you and I, and all the rest of us, started our lives. One goes with a heavy heart if we use these," he said, "because we are dealing with the seeds of the next generation."

He then addressed the second question: If embryos are going to be destroyed anyway, why not use them for research that might find cures? He noted the pro-life argument that "there is no such thing as excess life, and the fact that a living being is going to die does not justify experimenting on it or exploiting it as a natural resource." President Bush concluded his speech with this:

> At its core, this issue forces us to confront fundamental questions about the beginnings of life and the ends of science. It lives at a difficult moral intersection, juxtaposing the need to protect life in all its phases with the prospect of saving and improving life in all its stages.
>
> As the discoveries of modern science create tremendous hope, they also lay vast ethical mine fields. . . .
>
> Embryonic stem cell research is at the leading edge of a series of moral hazards. The initial stem cell researcher was at first reluctant to begin his research, fearing it might be used for human cloning. Scientists have already cloned a sheep.
>
> Researchers are telling us the next step could be to clone human beings to create individual designer stem cells, essentially to grow another you, to be available in case you need another heart or lung or liver. I strongly oppose human cloning, as do most Americans. We recoil at the idea of growing human beings for spare body parts or creating life for our convenience.
>
> And while we must devote enormous energy to conquering disease, it is equally important that we pay attention to the moral concerns raised by the new frontier of human embryo stem cell research. Even the most noble ends do not justify any means.
>
> My position on these issues is shaped by deeply held beliefs. I'm a strong supporter of science and technology, and believe they have the potential for incredible good—to improve lives, to save life, to conquer disease.

Research offers hope that millions of our loved ones may be cured of a disease and rid of their suffering. I have friends whose children suffer from juvenile diabetes. Nancy Reagan has written me about President Reagan's struggle with Alzheimer's. My own family has confronted the tragedy of childhood leukemia. And like all Americans, I have great hope for cures.

I also believe human life is a sacred gift from our Creator. I worry about a culture that devalues life, and believe as your President I have an important obligation to foster and encourage respect for life in America and throughout the world. . . .

As a result of private research, more than sixty genetically diverse stem cell lines already exist. They were created from embryos that have already been destroyed, and they have the ability to regenerate themselves indefinitely, creating ongoing opportunities for research.

I have concluded that we should allow federal funds to be used for research on these existing stem cell lines, where the life-and-death decision has already been made. . . . This allows us to explore the promise and potential of stem cell research without crossing a fundamental moral line by providing taxpayer funding that would sanction or encourage further destruction of human embryos that have at least the potential for life.

I also believe that great scientific progress can be made through aggressive federal funding of research on umbilical cord, placenta, adult, and animal stem cells, which do not involve the same moral dilemma. This year your government will spend $250 million on this important research.

As we go forward, I hope we will always be guided by both intellect and heart, by both our capabilities and our conscience.

I have made this decision with great care, and I pray it is the right one.

Thank you for listening. Good night, and God bless America.

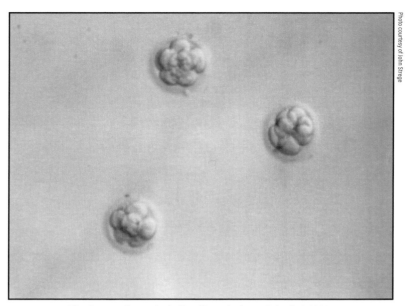

The three embryos, including Hannah, thawed, April 10, 1998.

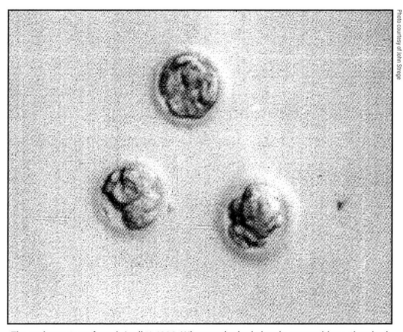

The embryos transferred, April 11, 1998. When we looked closely, we could see they had already gone to their next stage of development.

Rev. Dr. Charles Manske baptizes Hannah, April 1999.

Hannah at eight months old, August 1999.

Hannah's development from conception to two-year-old.

The Streges in Washington, DC, for Marlene's congressional testimony, 2001.

Hannah with Dr. James Dobson, when she sang "Jesus Loves the Little Children," 2001.

Hannah and Marlene enjoying the seaside, 2003.

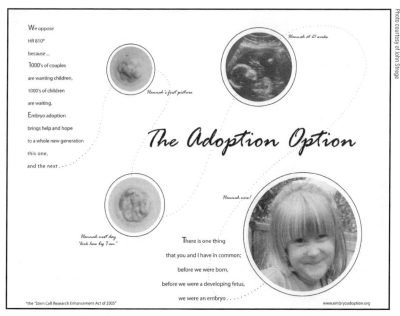

Hannah's poster given to Senator Barbara Boxer, 2004.

Hannah outside the West Wing of the White House, 2005.

Marlene and Hannah with Senator Sam Brownback, 2005.

Hannah in the Vermiel Room of the White House, 2006.

Hannah and Marlene under the presidential portrait of
Ronald Reagan in the White House, 2006.

Hannah and Marlene with President George W. Bush, 2006.

Hannah visits Dr. James Dobson at Family Talk, 2012.

Hannah, Marlene, and I were watching in a hotel room in Carlsbad, California. Moments after the president was done, we may have caused a minor commotion for those in the adjoining rooms. Hannah, meanwhile, knelt on the bed, folded her hands, and said a prayer of thanks. This was a victory, though it was also a compromise of sorts. Funding could go to research using the existing stem cell lines in which the embryos already had been destroyed. But the president had emphatically taken a stand on behalf of life by prohibiting the use of additional taxpayers' money for stem cell research that required further destruction of embryos.

Dr. Dobson's elation was palpable. Prior to the president's message, he had received a call from Karl Rove, his longtime friend and President Bush's senior adviser, informing him of the president's decision. He had already begun preparing to return to his radio studio, once Bush delivered his address, to record a program that would air the following day.

"I am incredibly relieved by George W. Bush's decision," he said on his radio show. "And I have to tell you, this is a miracle, folks. The pressure on the president in recent months to cave in on this issue had to have been immense. It is with a deep sigh of relief and, frankly, with great thankfulness to God because we've been praying about this. And I commend the president of the United States for making this brave decision."[3]

The "coincidental" timing of that broadcast airing on the day of President Bush's announcement was, well, supernatural, as described by both Dr. Dobson and Dr. Walt Larimore, vice president and family physician in residence at Focus on the Family.

"Some would call that a coincidence," Dr. Dobson said. "We know better. The Lord put us at this place at this time. I'm not sure why we did that program [that aired] on Thursday, but it was very obvious that the Lord was leading us in that direction."

Dr. Larimore summed it up perfectly. "The president stood at the crossroads of a culture of life and a culture of death, and he chose a culture of life. For all intents and purposes, he said life begins at conception. We will not sacrifice preborn human beings to benefit others. Their life is valuable. And that's a precept that occurs throughout Scripture from beginning to end."

This was not the end of it, of course. It never is in politics, notably with a compliant media. Jeffrey Kluger and Michael D. Lemonick, in the August 20, 2001, issue of *Time* magazine, were distressed by the president's decision.

> If President Bush hoped that his decision last week to permit limited federal funding of embryonic stem-cell research would quiet the ferocious debate surrounding the issue, it was a hope that was quickly dashed. Since his announcement, advocates on both sides have continued to find plenty to argue about— whether there are really 60 existing cell lines on which the President would allow research; whether those lines would be sufficient to yield real results; whether the restrictive rules will simply drive U.S. stem-cell researchers to other countries where they can do their work with less government interference.
>
> But nearly everyone agrees on one thing: stem cells, the unspecialized cells the body uses as raw material for tissues and organs, have the potential to treat an astonishing range of ills, including Parkinson's disease, diabetes, Alzheimer's and spinal-cord injuries. After Bush's decision, the question becomes whether they'll ever get a fair chance.[4]

Later that month, *Time* published a special issue, *America's Best Science and Medicine*. On the cover was a mugshot of Dr. James Thomson next to the headline: "The Man Who Brought You Stem Cells . . . Is One of America's Best in Science and Medicine." Beneath that was a smaller headline promoting another story: "Will the Bush Compromise Work?"[5]

CHAPTER 9

The Battle Continues

HANNAH WAS A typical child, though maybe one with friends in atypically high places. One day she was on her toy phone, talking to Dr. Dobson. She asked if he and Mrs. Dobson wanted to come to her birthday party. Then she spoke to President Bush and asked if he wanted to come. But like any other little girl, she also enjoyed playing dress up, caring for her dolls, and having us read books to her.

Two of her favorite books were *A Blessing from Above* by Patti Henderson and *Horton Hears a Who!* by Dr. Seuss, each pertinent to her own story. Here is the publisher's description of *A Blessing from Above*:

A beautiful story about adoption—and how each child is a blessing.
Every night before she goes to sleep, a kangaroo prays under the stars for a baby to love and hold. One day, as she rests under a tree, a baby bird falls out of its crowded nest—plop—right into her pouch!
Now, every night before they fall asleep, Momma-Roo and Little One thank God for all their blessings . . . but especially for each other.

As for *Horton Hears a Who!*, what child doesn't like Dr. Seuss books? We focused, as so many other pro-life parents have done over the years, on one simple but profound phrase: "A person's a person, no matter how small." This would not have met with approval from Theodor Geisel, aka Dr. Seuss, who by all accounts was pro-choice and disdained pro-life groups appropriating the phrase. "According to Seuss biographer Phil Nel, Geisel threatened to sue an anti-abortion rights group during the 1980s that used the statement on its stationery, forcing them to back down," ABC News's Marcus Baram wrote.[1]

Yet the phrase endured among pro-life groups. In a LifeNews.com story, "15 of the Greatest Pro-Life Quotes of All Time," Andrew Bair ranked the phrase second only to Ronald Reagan's quote: "I've noticed that everyone who is for abortion has already been born."[2]

We mean no disrespect toward the legacy of Dr. Seuss, whose work has been a household staple for generations of kids, including my own household when I was a child. But the phrase, notwithstanding its author and his intended audience, encapsulates simply and perfectly what an embryo is and helped us explain to Hannah her origins.

Several years later, Ron Stoddart, in *Christianity Today* magazine, wrote: "There are over 500,000 embryos currently frozen in storage at American clinics. Although together these embryos occupy a space the size of a 12mm cube—the size of a board game die—they represent the population of a city the size of Atlanta. Size is subject to perspective. We all look mighty small from the moon. But to God, we are wondrously made and valuable at every stage of development."[3]

Dr. Seuss and Ron Stoddart, one inadvertently and one purposely, made the case that these embryos, no matter how small—even as small as Senator Harkin's pencil dots—should not be destroyed for research purposes but instead should be given a chance at life by those willing to adopt them. Toward that end, President George W. Bush, in 2002, approved a Health and Human Services spending bill that included one million dollars for the Embryo Adoption Awareness Program, a series of grants that would promote embryo adoption and, by extension, prevent embryo destruction.

The following is from a notice by the Health and Human Services Department:

With the passage of Public Law 107-116, the FY 2002 Departments of Labor, Health and Human Services, Education and Related Agencies Appropriations Act, the Congress authorized the Secretary to conduct a public awareness campaign to educate Americans about the existence of frozen embryos available for adoption.

Senate Report 107-84 (page 244) contains the following statement:

"During hearings devoted to Stem Cell research, the Committee became aware of approximately 100,000 spare frozen embryos stored [in] in vitro fertilization (IVF) clinics throughout the United States. The Committee is also aware of many infertile couples who, if educated about the possibility, may choose to implant such embryos into the woman and, potentially, bear children. The Committee therefore directs the Department to launch a public awareness campaign to educate Americans about the existence of these spare embryos and adoption options. The Committee has provided $1,000,000 for this purpose."[4]

Curiously, and to his credit, it was championed by Senator Arlen Specter, who simultaneously was pro-life and pro-embryonic stem cell research. The cynical conclusion might be that he set out to prove frozen embryos would not be adopted in any notable numbers and hence would be destroyed anyway, so why not use them in research. Ronald Bailey, writing in *Reason* magazine, had a different theory, probably closer to the truth.

"Specter's effort to involve the feds in embryo adoption is a political maneuver to get him some cover on the embryonic stem cell issue," Bailey wrote. "Specter has been one of the leading congressional proponents of using stem cells derived from embryos for medical research aimed at eventually curing heart disease, Alzheimer's, diabetes, and other ills by creating perfect transplants. Stem cell research is being vigorously opposed by pro-life activists who argue that embryos are the moral equivalent of children. By proposing a federal embryo adoption promotion program, Specter is trying the hoary political tactic of being on both sides of an issue at once."[5]

Either way, Senator Specter deserves at least some credit. "If any of those embryos could produce life, I think they ought to produce life," he said. "Let us try to find people who will adopt embryos and take the necessary steps [to implant] them in women to produce life."[6]

It was unwelcome news for those in favor of embryonic stem cell research and for the pro-choice industry. Those who wanted federal funds for research that would destroy the embryos received none, while nearly one million dollars was allocated for the promotion of embryo adoption. Obviously, the gesture went unappreciated in many circles.

"Abortion-rights advocates worry that the program lays the legal groundwork for considering embryos human beings with full legal rights," Laura Meckler of the Associated Press wrote. "Using the term 'adoption' rather than 'donation' makes it appear that the program views embryos as children, said Kate Michelman, president of the National Abortion and Reproductive Rights Action League. If an embryo were a person with equal rights, abortion could be more easily declared illegal, she said."[7]

Michelman was not alone in this concern. An article titled "Pre Embryos: The Tiniest Speck of Potential Life Carrying the Seeds for Sweeping Change," in the University of Pittsburgh Law School's *Journal of Technology Law and Policy*, concludes: "Both the Embryo Adoption Awareness Campaign and the Secretary's Advisory Committee on Human Research Protections are viewed as the latest attempts by the Bush administration to undermine support for legal abortion and to erode efforts to fund embryo stem cell research."[8]

Meanwhile, Nightlight Christian Adoptions, as the agency that had introduced embryo adoption, was among those preparing a grant proposal, though it never had done one before.

"We just took it one step at a time and tried not to let the myriad requirements overwhelm us," Ron Stoddart said. "J. D. was indispensable for several reasons. She is a very bright person who was not easily intimidated. She provided a great source of optimism when we were getting discouraged by deadlines and regulations. She also was a good source of inspiration as we bounced ideas off of each other.

"It was very intimidating since Nightlight had never applied for a federal grant before, and we knew there would be bigger organizations standing in line to dine at the government trough. We just followed the instructions. We knew our overall goal was to bring embryo adoption into the mainstream, and that meant *lots* of publicity."

Its grant proposal was "an all of the above approach" to publicizing embryo adoption, Stoddart said. Nightlight proposed videos, direct mail to clinics and adoption agencies, and a website devoted exclusively to embryo adoption. "We knew we had a great story," he said.

Too many infertile couples were unaware then (and still are today) that there was such a thing as embryo adoption. The agency saw an opportunity to spread the word and was eager to do so. "I believe every embryo is a child that deserves a chance to be born," JoAnn Eiman told the Associated Press. "This is more than mere tissue. They need an option they haven't had in the past."[9]

When the grants were awarded, five hundred thousand dollars—half the allocated sum of one million dollars—was awarded to Nightlight Christian Adoptions.

"We were nobody," Stoddart said, "and then ended up getting the largest of the grants. J. D. was a godsend. She was just such a hard worker and did such a great job with it. We were overjoyed, to say the least. We knew we were the best bidder, but we were still surprised that we actually were recognized for our expertise."

Nightlight initially used the promotional funds to produce a series of videos, one of them written by Stoddart. It featured cryogenic tanks and children's voices.

"It's cold in here," one voice says.

"I know," another voice replies.

"What do you think is going to happen to us?"

"I don't know."

"Then it shows the couple holding the baby and oh, wow," Stoddart said. "All throughout this, my goal was for people to make the connection. Embryo, baby. There's no difference. It's a time line. Even the logo we use on the website that shows the embryo and then the early-developed fetus, the middle-developed fetus, and then the baby at the end. That line has always been to help people make the connection. Embryos, babies."

Though the connection is obvious, too many in the media and elsewhere disregarded it and considered it an obstacle to their goal of embryonic stem cell research funded by taxpayers, without regard to the progress made with adult stem cells. Possibly at play, too, was the media's general aversion to anything pro-life.

In his 2002 story for *National Review*, Wesley J. Smith, who has written extensively and passionately of his opposition to embryonic stem cell research, called out the media for its failure to acknowledge the progress made with adult stem cells, noting that it was "wearisome." He wrote: "When a research advance occurs with embryonic stem cells, the media usually give the story the brass-band treatment. However, when researchers announce even greater success using adult stem cells, the media reportage is generally about as intense and excited as a stifled yawn."[10]

On October 8, 2002, two pro-life congressmen, Mark Souder and Chris Smith, sent a letter to Elias Adam Zerhouni, MD, the director of the National Institutes of Health. It read in part:

> The Subcommittee has held a series of hearings on stem cell research and has been unable to identify a single patient who has been successfully treated with stem cells from either

embryos or embryo clones. We did, however, find a number of patients treated with stem cells from other courses. . . .

We have learned that more than 45 diseases are currently being treated with stem cells from cord blood. These include immune deficiencies and sickle cell. Likewise, adult stem cells have been used to successfully treat other medical conditions, from blindness to damaged heart tissue. . . .

Yet many in the media and scientific community have misrepresented the full potential of adult stem cells and exaggerated the applicability of embryonic stem cells and cloning. A September 5, 2002, Associated Press headline, for example, incorrectly proclaimed "Study: Adult Stem Cells Not Useful."[11]

Marlene began using a Lives Saved scoreboard, embryo adoption versus embryonic stem cell research. By the end of 2004, embryo adoption was leading, 81–0. Meanwhile, Do No Harm: The Coalition of Americans for Research Ethics began using its own scoreboard comparing treatments derived from adult stem cells versus embryonic stem cells. Adult stem cells opened up a 56–0 lead.

Alas, none of this mattered to the pro-embryonic stem cell research crowd. In November of 2004, the California Stem Cell Research and Cures Act, Proposition 71, appeared on the ballot in California as a response to President George W. Bush's disallowing federal funding for embryonic stem cell research. The proposition, if approved, would commit three billion dollars over ten years for stem cell research, with a high priority on embryonic stem cell research. It had widespread support and a mammoth gap in campaign contributions, 29 million dollars to 390,000 dollars raised by the opposition.

The liberal *San Francisco Chronicle* published a scathing rebuke to the proposition, written by Nigel M. de S. Cameron and Jennifer Lahl, who addressed the cloning issue that was included in the proposition.

In the annals of popular democracy, one of the strangest initiatives ever to make it to the ballot is the $3 billion bond known as Proposition 71. It is intended to sustain biotech researchers from the public purse while they pursue a project that private investors have already decided is worthless. And it is a project that nation after nation around the world has already declared to be a felony. . . .

Supporters of cloning for stem cells love to perpetuate the myth that their only opponents are crazy anti-abortion activists. That's plainly a lie; there is no other word for it. If it were true, why has all human cloning—including exactly the kind of research that the proposition would have us fund—been prohibited in Canada, under federal law? Why did Australia do the same thing? Why in Germany (where they know a thing or two about unethical research) will it get you five years in jail? Why is France on the verge of a similar law? None of these countries is in the grip of anti-abortion conservatives. Why is momentum building for a global convention to ban cloning at the United Nations?[12]

This was not hyperbole on the writers' part. When Proposition 71 passed with 59 percent of the vote, the *Los Angeles Times*, another leading liberal newspaper, wrote in its news story that the proposition

was designed to repudiate Bush's decision three years ago to greatly restrict the use of federal money for embryonic stem cell research. . . .

In addition to restricting federal money, Bush has twice backed measures in Congress that would have criminalized one type of embryonic stem cell research.

The bills, which have been blocked in the Senate, would impose prison sentences of 10 years and fines of $1 million for any type of cloning using human cells, including procedures that research advocates call therapeutic cloning.

Proposition 71 specifically earmarked money for therapeutic cloning, in which the DNA of an unfertilized egg is replaced with the DNA of an individual, producing stem cells that are a genetic match with the donor.

Researchers hope that cloned stem cells might allow scientists to study how diseases such as Alzheimer's develop. The work might also lead to treatments that would not be rejected by a patient's immune system.[13]

We were exceedingly disappointed, though not surprised, having lived in California for many years. In the heat of the moment, I said to Marlene, "We need to move." Cooler heads prevailed, though. When my niece heard of my threat to leave the state, she suggested we needed to stay put and carry on the fight.

She was right, of course. We weren't going anywhere, other than to Washington, DC—again. And again. And again.

CHAPTER 10

DC Lobbyists

"IT AIN'T OVER 'til it's over," Yogi Berra once said. So many of his renowned quotes, however baffling on the surface, made sense in their inimitable way. Another time he said of a popular restaurant, "Nobody goes there anymore. It's too crowded." Who can't relate to that?

But on the matter of when "it" is over, he was wrong on one front. It is never over in politics.

This is especially true of issues that many politicians and the mainstream media deem a threat to *Roe v. Wade*. Any suggestion that life begins at conception, though obviously true, sets off alarms among pro-choice factions. Thus, embryo adoption is viewed as a Trojan horse or a political wolf in sheep's clothing; calling it "adoption" rather than "donation" is seen as a cover for a nefarious effort to chip away at legalized abortion by giving the embryo full protection under the law.

We readily acknowledge that we find abortion reprehensible and morally wrong. But that was not why we chose the term embryo adoption or why we preferred "adoption" to "donation." According embryos the same respect as babies in a traditional adoption allows those placing the embryos to choose the adopting couples. There, too, are the safeguards—an FBI background check on the adopting couple and a home study ensuring that the adopting parents are responsible adults.

Yet as embryo adoption became a more familiar term with the introduction of the US Health and Human Services' new Embryo Adoption

Awareness Program, the mainstream media went to work attempting to discredit it.

A story in the *New York Times Magazine* called embryo adoption "a carefully chosen phrase" and embryo donation a "less loaded term."[1] A headline on an MSNBC story on August 20, 2002, noted "Bush to Promote 'Embryo Adoption.'" The quotation marks around "embryo adoption" are commonly called scare quotes, defined by *Merriam-Webster* as those "used to express especially skepticism or derision concerning the use of the enclosed word or phrase."[2]

"The procedure has been done for many years and everybody called it 'embryo donation,'" Dr. Eugene Katz, director of the Greater Baltimore Medical Center's Fertility Center, said to the Capital News Service. "Nobody called it 'embryo adoption.' It's politically driven."[3]

"It's interesting, the resistance from the people who don't want to call it adoption, who call it donation," Ron Stoddart said, "because [they say] you can only adopt a baby who's been born. How about the puppy down the street you adopted, or the highway that has been adopted? You don't have any problem with that. And there's no problem with doing a stepparent adoption, an international adoption, but an embryo adoption? Because that gives too much status to the embryo and it runs the risk of people starting to see that an embryo is a baby."

Yes, seeing an embryo for what it really is, a baby in its earliest stage of development. Dr. Katz was right, incidentally. The term was politically driven. But what was driving the politics was the fact that for those who favor embryonic stem cell research and want to convince others of its viability as a potential cure-all, it is far easier to say you support destroying an embryo for research purposes than it is to say you support destroying a baby.

Thus, the debate continued. In April 2004, fifty-eight senators, fourteen of whom were Republican, asked President Bush to reverse his position on funding embryonic stem cell research. Two hundred six members of the House of Representatives signed a letter urging

President Bush to reverse his position. Another letter, signed by 142 health associations and universities, was sent to President Bush urging him to expand federal funding for the research. He resolutely declined.

In June, a bill was introduced in Congress, H.R. 4682. "To amend the Public Health Service Act to provide for human embryonic stem cell research," it read. Section 1 of the bill said, "This Act may be cited as the 'Stem Cell Research Enhancement Act of 2004,'"[4] conveniently leaving off *embryonic*, as was often done, usually by the media. (Again, no one in our camp was opposed to stem cell research, only to research using stem cells from human embryos.)

It was a presidential election year, with Massachusetts senator John Kerry winning the Democratic nomination to oppose the incumbent George W. Bush. The Democratic National Convention in Boston in late July featured a speaker with a familiar name more closely associated with Republican politics: Ron Reagan, son of our forty-second president, Ronald Reagan, who had died less than two months earlier after suffering from Alzheimer's disease.

Reagan was there speaking on behalf of embryonic stem cell research and, by extension, Senator Kerry. Reagan was a Democrat and likely would have supported Kerry anyway. He had this to say:

> Good evening, ladies and gentlemen. A few of you may be surprised to see someone with my last name showing up to speak at a Democratic convention. Let me assure you, I am not here to make a political speech, and the topic at hand should not—must not—have anything to do with partisanship. I am here tonight to talk about the issue of research into what may be the greatest medical breakthrough in our or in any lifetime: the use of embryonic stem cells—cells created using the material of our own bodies—to cure a wide range of fatal and debilitating illnesses: Parkinson's disease, multiple sclerosis, diabetes, lymphoma, spinal cord injuries, and much more. . . .

Now, there are those who would stand in the way of this remarkable future, who would deny the federal funding so crucial to basic research. They argue that interfering with the development of even the earliest stage embryo, even one that will never be implanted in a womb and will never develop into an actual fetus, is tantamount to murder. A few of these folks, needless to say, are just grinding a political axe and they should be ashamed of themselves. But many are well-meaning and sincere. Their belief is just that, an article of faith, and they are entitled to it.

But it does not follow that the theology of a few should be allowed to forestall the health and well-being of the many. And how can we affirm life if we abandon those whose own lives are so desperately at risk? . . .

The tide of history is with us. Like all generations who have come before ours, we are motivated by a thirst for knowledge and compelled to see others in need as fellow angels on an often-difficult path, deserving of our compassion. In a few months, we will face a choice. Yes, between two candidates and two parties, but more than that. We have a chance to take a giant stride forward for the good of all humanity. We can choose between the future and the past, between reason and ignorance, between true compassion and mere ideology. This is our moment, and we must not falter. Whatever else you do come November 2nd, I urge you, please, cast a vote for embryonic stem cell research. Thank you for your time.[5]

This was what President Bush and a growing number of us were up against on this issue. Meanwhile, H.R. 4682 was referred to the Subcommittee on Health. Pressure continued to mount on the president, however, and soon Marlene and I, along with five-year-old Hannah, were headed back to Washington, DC—though initially not to lobby

politicians. Nightlight Christian Adoptions was among the organizations and individuals chosen by the Congressional Coalition for Adoptions to receive Angels in Adoption Awards at its annual banquet in
September. Ron Stoddart invited us to attend the banquet.

Marlene, ever vigilant in keeping Focus on the Family informed on
all things related to embryo adoption, let our friend Carrie Gordon Earll
know that we were returning to Washington. Carrie, the senior policy
analyst for bioethics at Focus on the Family, was aware of the ongoing
effort to pry money from federal coffers for embryonic stem cell research.
She saw an opportunity to continue our lobbying efforts in opposition.
Additional Snowflake families agreed to make the trip along with Ron
and Linda Stoddart and Marlene, Hannah, and me. Three days before
our departure, Carrie contacted Marlene and asked if she could set up a
meeting with one of California's senators, Barbara Boxer (D) or Dianne
Feinstein (D), since many of us were from California.

Marlene thought this likely was a nonstarter at such a late date until
she learned Boxer was involved with Angels in Adoptions. She commu-
nicated to Senator Boxer's staff why we were going to Washington—to
support adoption and a California adoption agency, Nightlight Christian Adoptions—and that we wished to thank her for supporting adoption. Thus a meet-and-greet for Senator Boxer was arranged with the
five California families who were part of our contingent.

Senator Boxer held extreme abortion positions. She also was wholly
in favor of embryonic stem cell research, noting as such in a Senate
debate a month before our trip to Washington.

"Boxer condemned President Bush's restrictions on the use of federal
funds for embryonic stem cell research as blocking potential medical
breakthroughs in curing diseases such as Alzheimer's and Parkinson's,"
the *San Diego Union-Tribune* wrote. "'Stem cell research is a crucial
issue of our time,' she said. She also criticized the California Republican
Party for going on record last weekend in opposition to Proposition 71
on the Nov. 2 ballot for embryonic stem cell research."[6]

One of the mothers in our group, a graphic artist, created posters featuring each of the five Snowflake children, showing photos of them as embryos and as kids. In the midst of the photos were the words "The Adoption Option."

"We oppose H.R. 4682 because thousands of couples are wanting children, thousands of children are waiting," the copy on the posters read. "Embryo adoption brings help and hope to a whole new generation. . . . There is one thing that you and I have in common. Before we were born, before we were a developing fetus, we were an embryo."

We had agreed it was not to be a contentious meeting with Senator Boxer. We would keep it cordial and upbeat while still making a point. When we finally met, Hannah presented Senator Boxer with her poster, while the parents of the other Snowflake babies gave her their posters. After a short conversation with Senator Boxer, photographs were taken. We were under no illusions that we might change Senator Boxer's mind, but we wanted her to know and see firsthand the results of frozen embryos being adopted, rather than destroyed for research purposes.

During our two days in Washington, we participated in seven news conferences, visited members of Congress in their offices, met with Senator Boxer, and made it onto the grounds of the White House at the Eisenhower Executive Office Building. There we met with White House officials, including Tim Goeglein, special assistant to President George W. Bush, and attended the Angels in Adoption Awards dinner. The group had done what it could to get its message across: that life begins at conception, and therefore embryos should not be destroyed; embryo adoption was a better option.

After we returned home, Hannah said to Marlene one morning before school, "Mommy, President Bush really does love children, doesn't he?" A few days later, while overhearing a Focus on the Family radio broadcast, she said the same about Dr. Dobson. "But you know who loves children the most?" Hannah asked.

"Who?"

"Jesus," she replied.

Yes, as the song goes, Jesus loves the little children.

Some surely would accuse us of having used our children as unwitting pawns. We would counter that we were instilling in them Christian values and the importance of standing up for your principles, including the sanctity of human life.

❄

Senator Kerry, meanwhile, took to bashing the president's stance against providing federal funds for embryonic stem cell research. Kerry "accused President Bush of 'turning his back on science in favor of ideology,' and he presented himself as the more forward-looking leader who would lift the president's restrictions on embryonic stem cell research," Jodi Wilgoren of the *New York Times* wrote.[7]

Kerry, appearing at a town hall meeting in Hampton, New Hampshire, said, "Now we stand at the edge of the next great frontier, but instead of leading the way, we're stuck on the sidelines. President Bush just doesn't get it. Faced with the facts, he turns away. Time and time again, he's proven that he's stubborn, out of touch, he's unwilling to change, he's unwilling to change course."

Wilgoren reported that the Kerry campaign began running an ad on Bush's opposition to embryonic stem cell research. "I believe that science can bring hope to our families," Kerry said in the ad. His campaign manager, Stephanie Cutter, called it "the sleeper issue of the campaign."

President Bush won reelection, but that did not mean the "sleeper issue" would be put to bed. Those in opposition to President Bush on this issue redoubled their efforts to have the government—taxpayers—fund research that so many found morally repugnant.

In February of 2005, Congressman Michael Castle (R-Delaware) introduced a new bill, H.R. 810 (replacing H.R. 4682), the Stem Cell Research Enhancement Act of 2005. On May 12, we received an email from Congressman Joe Pitts (R-Pennsylvania), as did Nightlight Christian Adoptions. Pitts was interested in arranging a news conference in Washington featuring Snowflake families in advance of the House of Representatives vote on H.R. 810 scheduled for May 24.

Marlene sent an email to Snowflake families, seeking volunteers to go to Washington. She wrote, "They are asking for Snowflake adoptive families in any stage of the Snowflake adoption process . . . [those who] just sent your application in; awaiting to be matched; just had a transfer, pregnant, or with born Snowflakes. This is a wonderful opportunity to once again let the world know that these are children that we are talking about, not cells for scientists to kill and dissect."

Marlene also received a request from the office of Tim Goeglein, special assistant to President Bush and deputy director of the White House Office of Public Liaison. Mr. Goeglein wanted Marlene to supply him with our reasons for supporting President Bush's existing policy on embryonic stem cell research and his decision not to provide federal funding for it in 2001. Marlene's extensive explanation included a point she often has made, which stood out for me:

"I was asked once by a science writer why I thought these embryos were human life. I said, 'Well, if they're not human life I would have had to add something [unusual] to make them a human life. You're the science writer. You tell me what I added.' No one has been able to answer that question. The medical answer is that all I added was oxygen, nutrients, a warm place to grow, and love . . . the same basic needs my daughter requires now!"

A few days later, we received the following note from Mr. Goeglein on White House stationery:

Dear Marlene and John:
    Thanks for sending that remarkable, and remarkably substantive, letter. Your story is remarkable, and so is your conviction.

I will share your views widely here as policy is formulated. Warm blessings to you and yours.

Tim Goeglein
Special Assistant to the President & Deputy Director of Public Liaison

Impressively, a group of eighty people from adopting and genetic families from all walks of life, including twenty-three Snowflake children (counting a set of yet-unborn twins), chose to make the trip to Washington with less than two weeks' notice. Their mission: to lobby members of Congress and make a united stand on behalf of the sanctity of life.

I stayed home to work, but Marlene and Hannah were again on a plane headed back to Washington. On May 23, 2005, they and others visited about a dozen congressmen and congresswomen to lobby against H.R. 810. That morning, Hannah, six at the time, said, "Mommy, I want to say something to them."

"Okay, Hannah, what do you want to say?"

"Don't kill the Snowflakes. We're kids and we want to grow up."

Kids—thankfully, in this case—do not have the capacity for nuance to obscure the truth.

The following morning, on the day of the vote, Marlene met with Representatives Mike Pence (R-Indiana) and Pitts and told them of Hannah's request. Pitts related the story in his opening comments at a news conference at the Capitol that morning. Early in the afternoon, when Marlene and Hannah met President Bush at the White House, she told him the story too.

"Oh, I heard that this morning on Marine One when I was traveling with a congressman," the president said.

The Snowflake families had been invited to the White House. When they arrived, they were escorted into the State Dining Room. Marlene was carrying two coats—Hannah's and hers—her purse, and a camcorder, and she was attempting to take in the whole scene—the large portrait of Abraham Lincoln over the fireplace and the floor-to-ceiling velvet draperies. Meanwhile she lost sight of Hannah, who already had befriended some of the other kids. Finally she spotted her peeking out from behind the draperies. She was going to go over and scold her. Instead she got out her camcorder. Just then, Hannah and a few other kids unwound from the draperies. Hannah raced over to Marlene and said, "Mommy, we're playing White House hide-and-seek."

Moments later, they went to the window and watched Marine One land on the White House lawn. President Bush soon met with the families, and when Marlene and Hannah were posing for a photo with the president, Marlene informed him that Hannah was the first Snowflake baby. The president took a step back, looked at Hannah, and said, "The pioneer."

The families were soon ushered into the East Room of the White House, where President Bush delivered his prepared remarks, discussing embryo adoption as an alternative to destroying embryos by using them in research.

"I have just met with twenty-one remarkable families," President Bush said to open his remarks.

> Each of them has answered the call to ensure that our society's most vulnerable members are protected and defended at every stage of life. The families here today have either adopted or given up for adoption frozen embryos that remained after fertility treatments. Rather than discard these embryos created during in vitro fertilization, or turn them over for research that destroys them, these families have chosen a life-affirming alternative. Twenty-one children here today found a chance for life with loving parents.
>
> I believe America must pursue the tremendous possibilities

of science, and I believe we can do so while still fostering and encouraging respect for human life in all its stages. In the complex debate over embryonic stem cell research, we must remember that real human lives are involved—both the lives of those with diseases that might find cures from this research, and the lives of the embryos that will be destroyed in the process.

The children here today are reminders that every human life is a precious gift of matchless value.[8]

President Bush expressed appreciation for Mike Leavitt, Secretary of Health and Human Services, who was in attendance, then saluted our friend and adoption attorney Ron Stoddart. "I want to thank the executive director of Nightlight Christian Adoptions, Ron Stoddart, for joining us today. Welcome. I want to thank Lori Maze, the director of Snowflakes Frozen Embryo Adoption program. Welcome, Lori. Thank you for coming. And thank you all for being here."

He recounted his policy set forth in 2001, one that "set a clear standard. We should not use public money to support the further destruction of human life." He continued:

Today, the House of Representatives is considering a bill that violates the clear standard I set four years ago. This bill would take us across a critical ethical line by creating new incentives for the ongoing destruction of emerging human life. . . .

Even now researchers are exploring alternative sources of stem cells, such as adult bone marrow and umbilical cord blood, as well as different ethical ways of getting the same kind of cells now taken from embryos without violating human life or dignity. With the right policies and the right techniques, we can pursue scientific progress while still fulfilling our moral duties.

I want to thank Nightlight Christian Adoptions for their

good work. Nightlight's embryo adoption program has now matched over two hundred biological parents with about one hundred forty adoptive families, resulting in the birth of eighty-one children so far, with more on the way.

The children here today remind us that there is no such thing as a spare embryo. Every embryo is unique and genetically complete, like every other human being. And each of us started out our life this way. These lives are not raw material to be exploited, but gifts. And I commend each of the families here today for accepting the gift of these children and offering them the gift of your love.

Once again, President Bush, a Christian man with pro-life convictions, followed his faith and his heart and stood his ground.

Marlene and Hannah returned to the Capitol later in the afternoon to listen to some of the debate before the vote took place. Rep. Trent Franks (R-Arizona) took Hannah and another Snowflake, nineteen-month-old Ella, onto the House floor and introduced them to other representatives while Marlene and Ella's mother, Meredith Gray, watched from the gallery above. We were told that this helped swing some votes against federal funding of embryonic stem cell research.

Not among them, unfortunately, was the vote cast by Darrell Issa, our own congressman from California's forty-ninth congressional district; his was among the 234 yea votes to the 194 nays. A pro-life Republican, Issa explained to Marlene and another Snowflake family that he was not yet decided, calling the matter "a conundrum." But later we learned the truth. Former first lady Nancy Reagan, a proponent of embryonic stem cell research, had been lobbying senators and representatives to support the bill. "Issa, who said he already had made up his mind to vote for the House bill last year [2004], said he got a call from her seeking advice on strategy," Associated Press writer Laurie Kellman wrote.[9]

Politicians call Issa's words to Marlene "obfuscation"; we prefer a simpler, more accurate word. He *lied*. He had already made up his mind. We never voted for Issa again.

His betrayal did not detract from an otherwise memorable trip for Marlene and Hannah. And the presence of the Snowflake children and their parents in Washington, their lobbying efforts, and the ensuing media coverage kept the vote from reaching the threshold necessary to override a presidential veto. Next up was a Senate vote.

❄

When Marlene and Hannah returned home, we were concerned that Hannah had understood, to the best of a six-year-old's ability, what this complex issue had been about and that it may have frightened her. When President Bush used the word *destroy* in his speech, Hannah had turned to Marlene and whispered, "Are they going to destroy me?" Marlene assured her they would not.

At home, as Marlene probed our daughter's grasp of the issue, Hannah responded simply but profoundly. "Mommy," she said, "you don't do experiments on babies. You don't kill babies!"

She decided to draw up a few posters, one to send to President Bush, another for Dr. Dobson, because "you both like Snowflakes." She wrote on the top of each, "We're kids," and "I love you," with XOXOXOX (hugs and kisses) at the bottom. She also drew a picture of three embryos. One represented herself, smiling because "she was adopted." The second featured a sad face because "he is still waiting for a mommy and daddy to get him." The third was saying, "Hmm . . . are you going to kill me?"

❄

More trouble was brewing in Washington, DC. On July 29, 2005, Senate Majority Leader Bill Frist (R-Tennessee) announced in a speech in the Senate that he would be supporting H.R. 810, the Stem Cell Research Enhancement Act.

"I am pro-life. I believe human life begins at conception," Frist, a physician, said.

> It is at this moment that the organism is complete—yes, immature—but complete. An embryo is nascent human life. It's genetically distinct. And it's biologically human. . . . And accordingly, the human embryo has moral significance and moral worth. It deserves to be treated with the utmost dignity and respect. I also believe that embryonic stem cell research should be encouraged and supported. . . .
>
> While human embryonic stem cell research is still at a very early stage, the limitation put into place in 2001 will, over time, slow our ability to bring potential new treatments for certain diseases. . . . Therefore, I believe the president's policy should be modified. We should expand federal funding . . . and current guidelines governing stem cell research, carefully and thoughtfully, staying within ethical bounds.[10]

He was rebuked immediately and widely by Christian leaders across the country. Tony Perkins, president of the Family Research Council, called the speech "very disappointing" and said Frist "was capitulating to the bio-tech industry."[11]

Dr. Dobson predictably was irate. Frist reportedly was considering a run for the presidency in 2008, and many believed he had taken his stated position for political expediency, seeking the middle ground on a complex issue. In a statement, Dr. Dobson said:

> It is an understatement to say that the pro-life community is disappointed by Sen. Frist's decision to join efforts to void President Bush's policy limiting the funding of embryonic

stem-cell research. Most distressing is that, in making his announcement, Sen. Frist calls himself a defender of the sanctity of human life—even though the research he now advocates results, without exception, in the destruction of human life. . . .

The media have already begun speculating that Sen. Frist's announcement today is designed to improve his chances of winning the White House in 2008 should he choose to run. If that is the case, he has gravely miscalculated. To push for the expansion of this suspect and unethical science will be rightly seen by America's values voters as the worst kind of betrayal—choosing politics over principle.[12]

Dr. Dobson, with his worldwide influence, was our greatest ally, but more importantly, an ally to all those children waiting to be born.

In August 2005, we were back in Colorado, again for the International, the PGA Tour event at Castle Pines Golf Club south of Denver. Per our custom, we paid a visit to Focus on the Family headquarters and, as usual, had to sign in at the reception desk and receive name badges.

"Why do I have to wear a badge?" Hannah asked. "Dr. Dobson knows who I am."

The comment found its way to Dr. Dobson's office ahead of us. When we walked in to greet him, Dr. Dobson said, "Hannah, take that badge off. I know who you are. Let's put it on your doll. I don't know who she is."

Dr. Dobson was disarmingly gentle and friendly with kids, his affection genuine. An athletic six feet, two inches tall, he could have been intimidating to a small child, but it was always immediately apparent that he loves children and they love him.

I say athletic because he is an avid sports fan who used to play pickup basketball games. I once asked him about his playing in one particular game, three-on-three, with the legendary "Pistol Pete" Maravich in the gymnasium at First Church of the Nazarene in Pasadena, California, on the day Maravich died in 1988 at age forty. Maravich, a Christian, had come to town to record a radio show with Dr. Dobson when Focus on the Family was still located in nearby Pomona. Dr. Dobson told me the story of how Maravich, during a break in their games, collapsed and died in his arms. He still got emotional in recalling it.

Dr. Dobson used the occasion of our visit to again record a radio program with Marlene, this time along with Claude Allen, President Bush's assistant for domestic policy. Allen had been involved in the event in the East Room of the White House in May. "It was the coming together of a very important event that we saw an opportunity, the need to put a message, to put a face to the president's policy as it relates to stem cell research and why the president has been so strong in not supporting embryonic stem cell research that destroys life," Allen said.[13]

"It was powerful. For the first time, the American public was able to see that the argument that these embryos that had been frozen were destined for destruction and had no purpose whatsoever [was false, because] standing before them were twenty-one beautiful, squirming, laughing, playing, crying, bottle-dropping children here in the East Room of the White House. It was a powerful event."

In the midst of President Bush's speech, Hannah, six at the time, had become concerned with what President Bush might be saying. Afterward, as they were leaving the East Room to head to another room for the birthday celebration, Allen overheard Marlene and Hannah talking.

"I just happened to be standing and observing and [Marlene] was trying to explain what was going on in the East Room of the White House," Allen said, "and Hannah turned and said, 'Is that man going to kill me?' And Marlene turned to Hannah and said, 'No, Hannah. That's the president, and he's here to protect you.' And that just ripped me to hear that, to hear a child crying out for life and to know there's someone there who's standing to protect him or her and it's our president. And he's standing to protect these Snowflakes to give them an opportunity at life, so that we don't need to destroy embryos that can be given life by families that choose to adopt them through the Snowflake program."

"All her life," Marlene replied, "she's only known Snowflakes as, these are her friends and these are her. We're at the White House, and I can just imagine what she's thinking. She sees these military in their dress uniforms and [hears] the president's speech, probably talking about destroying embryos, and she turns to me and says, 'Mommy, are they going to destroy me?'"

❊

Our visits with Dr. Dobson and others at Focus on the Family were always cathartic. They allowed us to destress and be reminded that God is in control while also reinforcing our commitment to protecting frozen embryos. The controversy was not going away anytime soon, and the side we steadfastly continued to support still needed advocates and those young faces as reminders of what was at stake.

Embryo adoption and protecting frozen embryos were also important because of cultural opposition that went beyond disagreement to mockery, long before Twitter gave everyone a platform to mock away. In November of 2005, the television show, *CSI: Crime Scene Investigation*, aired an episode it called "Secrets and Flies." We have never watched much network television (other than my watching sports). We have never seen a single episode of any CSI show, so obviously we had not seen this one.

The plot, according to Catholic League for Religious and Civil Rights, "revolves around the murder of Christina, a single mother. After an autopsy reveals that Christina was a virgin, it is learned that she adopted a fertilized embryo from Project Sunflower, an organization devoted to finding surrogate mothers for abandoned embryos."[14]

Sunflower babies.

Reviews from the Christian community and our circle found the show unfavorable at best and disturbing at worst. Here are some of the remarks from Bill Donahue, president of the Catholic League for Religious and Civil Rights:

> CSI chose to advance a pro-abortion rights agenda by portraying those who are opposed to abortion as religious nuts not to be taken seriously. The murder victim, who gave life to a baby who would otherwise be left to die, is described as a "prude" for being chaste. A remark is made about her being "our virgin Mary."
>
> According to the CSI website, the doctor in charge of Project Sunflower is "a very unlikable woman." The pro-abortion rights forensic investigators sneer at her work and beliefs, informing us that a pope once decreed that a baby isn't a human until quickening. (Of course, it is not explained that the Church has always considered abortion to be illicit, regardless of the status of the baby. Never mind the fact that we have learned a few new things about biology in a few hundred years.)[15]

In the three previous years, the show was number one in the Nielsen ratings and in 2005 it was ranked third. It was a highly acclaimed, award-winning show with an enormous audience.

It would not be the last of the animus directed toward embryo adoption and the Christians who support it.

❄

News of embryo adoption continued to spread, even beyond America's borders. A writer for *Marie Claire* magazine, for instance, was interested in doing a story. She called Marlene from France and said she'd been

told that "Hannah knows everything" about her adoption and wanted
to know if that was true. Marlene explained that she knew about it
to the extent that a six-year-old could understand, namely, that she
was adopted and that it was a good thing. The writer asked whether
Hannah knew what adoption meant. Marlene was not quite sure, so on
the way to school the following morning, she asked.

"Hey, Hannah, do you know what the word *adoption* means, or *to
adopt?*"

Hannah, in her car seat in the back, began thinking about it. Finally
she had the answer.

"Love!" she said.

"That's exactly right," Marlene told Hannah.

"I wanted to cry," Marlene said later.

"I just felt so overwhelmed," she wrote in an email to Carrie Gordon
Earll at Focus on the Family, "because whenever we talk about adoption, we always mention that God adopted all three of us into his family, through Jesus on the cross. I just felt the significance of her answer
with regards to our salvation."

However acrimonious the debate was going to get, we would be
okay.

In October of 2005, my latest book, *When War Played Through: Golf
During World War II*, was published. At Marlene's insistence, we sent
a copy to President Bush, who was an avid golfer from a family with a
long history of golfers. His great-grandfather, George Herbert Walker,
and grandfather, Prescott Bush, had both served as president of the
United States Golf Association.

Just before Christmas, we received yet another letter from the White
House:

Dear Marlene and John:

   Thank you for the card and inscribed copy of *When War
Played Through*. I appreciate your thoughtfulness. Thanks as

well for making the trip to Washington back in May. It was a pleasure to welcome you to the White House.

Laura and I send our best wishes for a joyous holiday season.

Sincerely,
George W. Bush

It was encouraging to know that on this contentious issue of embryonic stem cell research, our expanding group of Christian families that had adopted frozen embryos had an advocate in the Oval Office, one who was taking an ethical and moral stand and steadfastly refusing to bow to political pressure.

Yes, we were all going to be okay.

CHAPTER 11

Thank You, Mr. President

HANNAH CELEBRATED HER seventh birthday on December 31, 2005, though her birthday party was delayed for a month or so. Most of her friends were from her first-grade class at Zion Lutheran School, and all the girls had been invited. We had ample space behind our home, and we hired a man with a pony to come over and give the girls pony rides, naively failing to consider the precedent we were setting, that each ensuing birthday party would be expected to outdo the previous one. Realistically, it was going to be downhill for her parties from there on out.

The point is that she was enjoying a normal childhood, with a few notable exceptions—all related to her story—including her already having met the president of the United States in the White House. In April, Hannah announced to Marlene, "I want to write a book about Snowflakes, and I want Daddy to help publish it, and I want you to help me illustrate it." As it turned out, the story was still unfolding.

Less than three months later, word came down that yet another trip to Washington, DC, was in the offing. H.R. 810, the Stem Cell Research Enhancement Act of 2005, already passed by the House in 2005, was being taken up by the Senate and would soon be put to a vote, notwithstanding the likelihood that President Bush would veto it.

On June 7, 2006, Rep. Mike Castle (R-Delaware), the sponsor of the bill, and Rep. Diana DeGette (D-Colorado) requested a meeting with the president to discuss the issue. They were denied.

"It's regrettable that President Bush will not even grant us the common courtesy of a meeting to discuss stem cell research," DeGette told CBS News. "However, it's downright insulting that, at the same time, he sent his head political adviser to my hometown with a veto threat."[1]

She was referring to Karl Rove, deputy chief of staff to the president, and it was not a threat. Rove had told the *Denver Post*'s editorial board that should the Senate approve the bill, the president would veto it. "The president is emphatic about this," Rove told the newspaper.[2]

Nightlight Christian Adoptions, meanwhile, was contacted about assembling a group of Snowflake families, once more on short notice, to come to Washington to represent the embryo adoption side of the issue and lend support to President Bush. The response was remarkable— twenty or so families from California, Washington, Maryland, Pennsylvania, Virginia, Michigan, Arizona, North Carolina, and Texas agreed to interrupt their lives, take time off from work, and tap into savings accounts to pay for the trip. The opportunity to visit the White House is always a strong inducement, of course, but this was about so much more than that. These families went because they were passionate about the cause and embraced the opportunity to stand together and make a statement on behalf of life.

They weren't there strictly for show either. They were encouraged to lobby the representatives from their areas, many of whom were in favor of H.R. 810—including, sadly, our own congressman, Darrell Issa. It was a formidable group, especially with kids in tow, from infants to our own seven-year-old. When kids are involved, the target is not nearly as enticing.

On July 17, 2006, the Senate began its debate in advance of its vote on H.R. 810. Senator Sam Brownback (R-Kansas) was among those arguing against the bill, and in so doing proved himself a star in our growing galaxy. He came armed with visuals, including a chart of photos made a few years earlier that showed Hannah at every stage of development, from an embryo on the day of thawing, to the following day when she had moved on to her next stage of development, to an ultrasound a few months later, then the day of her birth, and on into childhood.

"This is a particular young person, a young girl named Hannah that I just met with a few hours ago," Brownback said.[3] "This is when she was adopted as a frozen embryo, and this shows her development taking place. If you destroy her here"—he pointed to the photo of her as an embryo—"you don't get her here," he said, pointing to her as a little girl at two and a half. "That is the key. She was called a Snowflake, an adopted frozen embryo. I hope that some who are maybe watching or hear about this, if they have frozen human embryos, they consider putting them up for adoption, because a number of people want to adopt them."

He moved on to the drawing Hannah had made the previous year, with the words, "We're kids. I love you."

"Then she draws three pictures here below," Brownback said. "This is her smiling because she got adopted and she's here. Here is another frozen embryo that's sad because he's still sitting in a frozen state, and then here's one that as she explains is saying, 'What, are you going to kill me?' This was her explanation to her mother that just gave this chart to me."

Out of the mouths of babes comes great wisdom, as the senator said about Hannah's contributions. This was Hannah's rudimentary, yet illuminating, understanding of the stakes.

"I hope people really think about that," Senator Brownback said. "This is not just a clump of tissue. This is not just a group of a few cells. This is not a hair follicle. This is not a fingernail. This is Hannah. And if nurtured grows to be just this beautiful child, and we got a lot of them, of frozen embryos. And I hope people will consider putting them up for adoption, because there's a lot of people that want to adopt them."

The opinion media generally saw it differently. Dana Milbank, in the *Washington Post*, wrote:

George W. Bush has signed 1,116 consecutive bills into law since becoming president. He probably wishes he had vetoed just one of them.

Instead, Bush faces the prospect of casting his first veto this week against embryonic stem cell research, defying the wishes not just of a majority of Americans and their representatives but also of Nancy Reagan and those representing millions of people with Parkinson's disease, diabetes, spinal injuries and the like . . .

Brownback, beneath an oil portrait of George Washington, beckoned to a photograph of a bald eagle and complained of a disparity between treatment of human and bird embryos. "You can face . . . two years in prison for destroying a bald eagle egg," he said, but "taxpayer dollars are used to destroy a human at the same phase of life."[4]

Bloomberg News columnist Margaret Carlson later wrote:

The day before Tuesday's U.S. Senate vote backing embryonic stem cell research, Republican Sam Brownback appeared with several Snowflakes, the name given to children born from frozen embryos. It was a lovely tableau, proof of the wisdom of kissing every baby on the campaign trail.

With polls showing a large majority of Americans favoring federal funds for such research, Snowflakes are the last redoubt of a minority of a minority within the Republican Party adamantly opposed to it.[5]

She also called embryos "unimplanted specks—with the feelings, soul and brains of a gnat."

It is worth a reminder that embryonic stem cell research was not unlawful, was still being conducted, and had not remotely demonstrated that it might one day deliver on its "potential."

The Senate, as expected, voted in favor of H.R. 810, with sixty-three yeas and thirty-seven nays. The next morning, the bill, having been passed by both houses of Congress, was presented to President Bush, awaiting a signature that was not forthcoming. Per protocol, President Bush sent a written response to the House of Representatives, "returning herewith without my approval H.R. 810, the 'Stem Cell Research Enhancement Act of 2005.'"[6] He wrote:

> Like all Americans, I believe our Nation must vigorously pursue the tremendous possibilities that science offers to cure disease and improve the lives of millions. Yet, as science brings us ever closer to unlocking the secrets of human biology, it also offers temptations to manipulate human life and violate human dignity. Our conscience and history as a Nation demand that we resist this temptation. . . .
>
> Advances in research show that stem cell science can progress in an ethical way. . . . I hold to the principle that we can harness the promise of technology without becoming slaves to technology and ensure that science serves the cause of humanity. If we are to find the right ways to advance ethical medical research, we must also be willing when necessary to reject the wrong ways. For that reason, I must veto this bill.[7]

President Bush then went to the East Room of the White House, where the Snowflake families had assembled for his televised address explaining his veto. Joining the Snowflake families was the remarkable Joni Eareckson Tada, a quadriplegic from a diving accident in 1967. A devout Christian, prolific author, and the founder of Joni and Friends, a Christian disability ministry, Tada is steadfastly opposed to embryonic stem cell research, even though many scientists have argued it has the potential to cure her paralysis. In a 2003 article, she noted how often she was asked about Christopher Reeve and his advocacy on behalf of the research. "Don't I want a cure?" she said. "I would love to walk. But thirty-five years of quadriplegia since a diving accident in 1967 has honed my perspective. I look at the broader implications of medical research as a double-edged sword."[8]

Once again, I had stayed home to work. When President Bush strode to the podium, I was watching on the Fox News Channel with more than a little pride, seeing Marlene and Hannah sitting just behind the president and to the left of the podium.

President Bush did not disappoint. He explained his reasons for the veto and what the Snowflake children represented. "They remind us of what is lost when embryos are destroyed in the name of research," he said.

> They remind us that we all begin our lives as a small collection of cells. And they remind us that in our zeal for new treatments and cures, America must never abandon its fundamental morals.
>
> Some people argue that finding new cures for disease requires the destruction of human embryos like the ones that these families adopted. I disagree. I believe that with the right techniques and the right policies we can achieve scientific progress while living up to our ethical responsibilities. . . .
>
> If this bill would have become law, American taxpayers would, for the first time in our history, be compelled to fund the deliberate destruction of human embryos. And I'm not going to allow it. I made it clear to the Congress that I will not allow our nation to cross this moral line. . . . Crossing the line would needlessly encourage a conflict between science and ethics that can only do damage to both, and to our nation as a whole. If we're to find the right ways to advance ethical medical

research, we must also be willing, when necessary, to reject the wrong ways. So today, I'm keeping the promise I made to the American people by returning this bill to Congress with my veto.[9]

Thank you, Mr. President.

Joni Eareckson Tada, with whom Hannah had her photo taken beneath a portrait of Abraham Lincoln, saluted the president with this statement:

> I stand with countless Americans with disabilities who believe that our cause is not advanced when human life is sacrificed in hopes of finding a cure. People like me who are medically fragile are left vulnerable and exposed in a society that views human life as a commodity which can be experimented upon or exploited. Any research that destroys human embryos is an affront to God's creative authority.
>
> I am grateful for the principled stand our President has taken, first and foremost because of the sanctity of human life, but also because restrictions on use of taxpayer dollars may well encourage funding in the overlooked and less commercially-viable field of adult stem cell therapy.[10]

Later that day, representatives again assembled to debate H.R. 810, and another vote was called to see whether it could increase the number of yea votes to two-thirds. Could it do so, it would then return to the Senate to give senators a second chance to get to two-thirds in favor, which would override President Bush's veto.

New Jersey Congressman Chris Smith again passionately made a case against passing the bill, noting, among other issues, zero successes with embryonic stem cell research and the stunning breakthroughs and successes announced almost daily of adult and cord blood stem cell therapies that are today helping men and women with leukemia, sickle cell anemia, and a myriad of other diseases. . . .

Arguments were made on this floor, Mr. Speaker, that we are just using spare or leftover embryos as if they exist as a subclass of surplus human beings that can be experimented on or slaughtered at will. A few hours ago, at the White House, several of us met with some of those Snowflake children, all of whom were adopted while they were still in their embryonic stage and frozen in what we like to call frozen orphanages. Believe me, watching Snowflake children laugh, smile, and act, well, like kids underscored the fact that they are every bit as human and alive and precious as any other child. Under the Castle bill, these so-called surplus humans are throwaways. Adopt them, don't destroy them. . . .

Yesterday, Hannah Strege, the first known Snowflake embryo adopted, told a small group of us: "Don't kill the embryos, we are kids and we want to grow up too." How come a seven-year-old gets it and we don't? Sustain the veto.[11]

Thank you too, Congressman Smith.

When it was time for a vote, yeas again carried the day, 235 to 193 nays, but still did not meet the two-thirds threshold that would have sent it back to the Senate for reconsideration.

It is difficult to measure the effect the Snowflake families had on the debate, given the media bias working against us. But we can be reasonably certain our impact helped in a couple of ways. It gave President Bush cover for what was an unpopular stand in many circles, and it informed those who previously were unaware of the issues and what was at stake. Ron Stoddart, in a story on Nightlight's website, summed it up well.

To think that we had an impact on our nation's policies toward protecting life was pretty heady stuff. Twenty families responded to our last-minute call to begin their odyssey to our nation's capital along with their Snowflake children.

I'm sure that everyone has met a celebrity at one point in their life and you can't help but form impressions. This was certainly no different. George Bush was more than the President of the United States, surrounded by all of the trappings of power. He met with us as a man who understood and shared our deepest commitment to life. It was clear that to him this wasn't politics, it was principle. Diogenes should have visited the White House while Mr. Bush was President.[12]

Stands taken on principle over politics, notably those involving Christianity and pro-life conservatives, generally are not well received in the liberal media. Case in point: *Wonkette*, which self-identifies as a political gossip website started in 2004 by the now defunct Gawker Media. *Wonkette*'s then coeditor Alex Pareene wrote:

Oh christ [sic], we thought Brownback made that term up. "Snowflake babies" doesn't make sense as a metaphor! Do snowflakes develop into snowballs through some biological process previously unknown to us? Would using stem cells for research count as catching a flake on one's tongue or building a snow fort? What strategist thought up this term anyway? We could've come up with something way better. Like:
Kidsicles
TCBChildren
Frozen Souls
Abominable Snow Babies
Dippin' Tots—the Babies of the Future![13]

Liza Mundy, for the liberal magazine *Mother Jones*, wrote a story headlined "Souls on Ice" and included this passage on embryo adoption:

> Also known as "embryo donation," this is a process whereby embryos are relinquished by whoever created them and handed over to another couple, or person. In most states, this is essentially a property transfer, not an adoption, and advocates for the infertile, as well as old-line reproductive rights groups, fear the use of the word "adoption" is one more attempt to confer humanhood on the embryo, a backdoor anti-abortion sally. They are right: To dramatize his opposition to federal funding for stem cell research, Bush in May 2005 posed with a group of "Snowflakes" babies, children who started life as leftover IVF embryos and were donated to other couples, thanks to the brokerage of an explicitly Christian, explicitly pro-life embryo adoption group called Snowflakes.[14]

"A backdoor anti-abortion sally" was one more example of what we were routinely hearing from the media: that the ultimate goal of this movement was overturning *Roe v. Wade* or abolishing abortion altogether. We readily acknowledge our pro-life position. But not once throughout this entire process, from its inception in 1997 to President Bush's veto in 2006, had we ever heard anyone on the embryo adoption side—publicly or privately, public figures or private citizens—ever suggest that overturning *Roe v. Wade* was the endgame or even a means by which to weaken the abortion industry. This was a fabrication by the media.

So be it. The sanctity of human life was a cause worth fighting for, and President Bush understood this implicitly. Two weeks following his veto, we—and the other Snowflakes families, I'm sure—received a letter from the White House.

Dear Friends:

I was honored to welcome you to the White House to celebrate the value of life. You have answered a great calling, and your love and compassion are an inspiration to the American people. Your family reminds us that every human life is a precious gift.

Best wishes.

Sincerely,
George W. Bush

In August we made one more business trip to Colorado, this one for the International at Castle Pines Golf Club—the last one ever played. Again Marlene and Hannah came along, and again we paid a visit to Focus on the Family, along with friends, one of whom had her three boys with her. We were downstairs in the Kids' Korner, the play area at the Welcome Center, when Marlene asked if I could watch the three boys and Hannah while they went upstairs to the bookstore to shop. Of course I'd watch them. What could go wrong?

Several minutes later, Marlene heard an announcement over the loudspeaker. "Would parents please keep their children with them." Odd, Marlene thought. What kind of parents would leave their children unattended?

A few minutes later, Marlene overheard Hannah talking to our friend in the next aisle. "We can't find my daddy," Hannah said. "He left us in Odyssey and Whit's End, and we can't find him."

I had taken them into the Narnia room. I knew nothing about C. S. Lewis's fantasy novel *The Lion, the Witch and the Wardrobe* and had not seen the film. Hence, I had no idea about the wardrobe and its door to a secret world. The kids went through the wardrobe door and never came out. They'd exited through a back door of which I was unaware.

Marlene and the group came back downstairs looking for me and found me patiently waiting for the kids.

A month later, as school recommenced, Hannah's teacher asked the students to write about something exciting they had experienced over the summer. Here is what Hannah did *not* write about: going to the White House for the third time; meeting President George W. Bush for the second time; meeting Senators Sam Brownback, Bill Frist, and Chuck Schumer; or having Senator Brownback, on the floor of the Senate, call her "a pioneer" and display the poster she had made about embryos.

Here is what Hannah *did* write about: my losing the kids in Narnia at Focus on the Family.

CHAPTER 12

Playing Hardball

POLITICAL ADS IN the run-up to an election are ubiquitous, tiresome, and probably largely ignored. But this particular election season, two were impossible to overlook. They aired in Missouri during the 2006 World Series between the St. Louis Cardinals and Detroit Tigers. One of the ads even featured the Cardinals' starting pitcher in game four in St. Louis.

Missouri was in the midst of a Senate race, Claire McCaskill challenging incumbent Jim Talent. On its November ballot, it also had Amendment 2, the Missouri Stem Cell Research and Cures Initiative, which would allow embryonic stem cell research and therapeutic cloning (essentially cloning embryos that also would be destroyed for their stem cells). McCaskill was in favor; Talent opposed.

On McCaskill's side was Michael J. Fox, an outspoken advocate on behalf of embryonic stem cell research for its potential to cure Parkinson's, among other diseases. On October 22, during game two of the World Series, a thirty-second ad featuring Fox appeared in Missouri during the telecast of the game.

"In Missouri, you can elect Claire McCaskill, who shares my hope for cures," Fox said. "Unfortunately, Senator Jim Talent opposes expanding stem cell research."[1]

I will interrupt Fox here to note the deception in the ad. Talent opposed only embryonic stem cell research. The word *embryonic* was conveniently left out, as continued to be the case in this debate.

LifeNews.com called out Fox on this. "Though the ad makes it appear Talent opposes all kinds of stem cell research, he has voted in favor of spending millions in federal funds for adult stem cell research, the only kind of research that has ever cured a single patient. What Talent has opposed is forcing taxpayers to pay for studies using embryonic stem cells, which can only be obtained by destroying human life."[2]

But I digress.

"Senator Talent," Fox continued, "even wanted to criminalize the science that gives us a chance for hope. They say that all politics is local, but that's not always the case. What you do in Missouri matters to millions of Americans—Americans like me."[3]

The group Missourians Against Human Cloning, meanwhile, was preparing its own ad, but once the Fox ad appeared, it expedited production to have its counter ad ready to air on October 25, during the fourth game of the World Series. The starting pitcher for the Cardinals that night was Jeff Suppan, who also was appearing in the ad, along with actress Patricia Heaton from the television show *Everybody Loves Raymond*; actor Jim Caviezel, who portrayed Jesus in the film *The Passion of the Christ*; St. Louis Rams quarterback Kurt Warner; and Mike Sweeney of the Kansas City Royals.

"Amendment 2 claims to ban human cloning," Suppan said in the ad, "but in the two thousand words you won't read, it makes cloning a constitutional right."

Heaton, a Christian and strong pro-life advocate, said, "Amendment 2 actually makes it a constitutional right for fertility clinics to pay women for eggs. Low-income women will be seduced by big checks, and extracting donor eggs is an extremely complicated, dangerous, and painful procedure."[4]

There was no shortage of backlash on both sides. Fox was accused of exploiting his disease to help McCaskill win the election. Rush Limbaugh, meanwhile, accused Fox of exaggerating his condition, for which the talk radio icon later apologized. And Heaton told the *New*

York Times she was talked into recording a twelve-second segment for a fund-raising video for Amendment 2 that somehow made it into the ad. She also said she was unaware that Fox had done an ad in favor of McCaskill and, by extension, Amendment 2.

"Because of the timing, her comments looked like a response to his and became associated with Rush Limbaugh's suggestion that Mr. Fox was faking his symptoms for sympathy," the *New York Times*'s Jesse Green wrote. "Ms. Heaton was appalled, she said. 'Not only was the ad so bad, but why was it put on? It took the focus off of what we're talking about, which is very serious, and made it look like a feud or something, a Hollywood tabloid subject, a media thing of pitting people against each other.'"[5]

We have no reason to doubt Heaton's recollection of the events. She is a fearless advocate on behalf of pro-life causes. She was on the right side of this debate, though taking her at her word, she should not even have appeared in the ad.

Ultimately, however, it proved to be the winning side of the debate, notwithstanding Amendment 2 having been passed by Missourians by a narrow 2.4 percentage margin. In late 2005, in the run-up to the election, a poll showed Amendment 2 with 68 percent support. It took a few months before anyone realized that even though it passed, it was a loss, as Stephanie Simon noted in the *Los Angeles Times*:

> Unable to recruit top scientists, despite cutting-edge labs and an endowment of $2 billion, the Stowers Institute for Medical Research . . . canceled plans for a major expansion in Kansas City. The research institute also moved a large chunk of its endowment to Delaware, calling the political climate in Missouri too hostile for investment.
>
> "It's like Amendment 2 never passed," said Bill Duncan, president of a scientific consortium seeking to build a biotech hub here [in Kansas City].[6]

It was a small victory, but a victory nonetheless, and not an unimportant one. They all mattered. The pro-embryonic stem cell research side was relentless and required vigilance on our side to help counter it. States were bypassing the federal coffers and devoting their own taxpayers' funds toward the research, as California had done with its Proposition 71 in 2004. In 2005, the legislature in Connecticut committed one hundred million dollars over a ten-year period to embryonic and adult stem cell research, though the bulk of the award was earmarked for research on embryos. Later that year Illinois governor Rod Blagojevich, via executive order, launched the Illinois Regenerative Medicine Institute, using ten million dollars of public funds to kick-start it. New Jersey, New York, Iowa, Massachusetts, and Maryland also joined the parade.

The Senate and House of Representatives continued their pursuit of federal funding. They passed Senate Bill S.5, the Stem Cell Research Enhancement Act of 2007, though without enough votes to override a veto. On June 20, President Bush, as he said he would, vetoed the bill.

The following year, 2008, was a presidential election year, and in 2007 candidates were putting down their markers early—among them Senators Barack Obama (D-Illinois) and Hillary Clinton (D-New York), who were vying for the Democratic nomination for president.

Obama, during a debate on Senate Bill S.5, said, "I am frustrated by the opposition this bill has generated and saddened that we are preventing the advancement of important science that could potentially impact millions of suffering Americans. The study of stem cells holds enormous promise for the treatment of debilitating and life-threatening diseases. However, in order to reach this level of medical achievement, much more research is necessary to understand, and eventually harness, the amazing potential of stem cells. Instead of creating roadblocks, we must all work together to expand federal funding of stem cell research and continue moving forward in our fight against disease by advancing our knowledge through science and medicine."[7]

Clinton, speaking at the Carnegie Institution for Science, said,

The Bush administration has declared war on science. The record is breathtaking: banning the most promising kinds of stem cell research. . . .

When I am president, I will lift the current ban on ethical stem cell research. In 2001, President Bush issued an Executive Order banning federal funding for some of the most promising avenues of stem cell research. And this year—yet again—he vetoed legislation to open up new lines of embryonic stem cells for federal funding. Every day, we are learning more about the opportunities this kind of research offers. Within these cells may lie the cures for Parkinson's disease, Alzheimer's, spinal cord injuries, diabetes, Huntington's and more. One hundred million Americans live with these conditions—and their families live with them too. The president's ban on stem cell funding amounts to a ban on hope. It's as if these families are invisible to their president.[8]

On the Republican side, Senator John McCain (R-Arizona) was in favor of federal funding of embryonic stem cell research and had supported it in the past. In a debate between Republican candidates, he said, "I believe that we need to fund [embryonic stem cell research]. This is a tough issue for those of us in the pro-life community. I would remind you that these stem cells are either going to be discarded or perpetually frozen. We need to do what we can to relieve human suffering. It's a tough issue. I support federal funding."[9]

Mitt Romney, McCain's opponent, was straddling a fine line. He was against federal funding for embryonic stem cell research, yet he was fine with parents deciding to give up their embryos for research purposes. "I think before we move too far down that road," he said in an interview on NBC's *Meet the Press*, "that we establish a provision for parents to have authority over their own embryos and to have adoption procedures so that they might be able to provide these embryos, as some call them, Snowflake babies, to allow them to be adopted by others and to be implanted and become human beings. That's the course I'd prefer."[10]

It was getting tiresome.

Then came a story in the *New York Times* claiming, "Man Who Helped Start Stem Cell War May End It." That man was James A. Thomson, the University of Wisconsin scientist who "in 1998 plucked stem cells from human embryos for the first time, destroying the embryos in the process and touching off a divisive national debate." Now, nine years later, "his laboratory was one of two that reported a new way to turn ordinary human skin cells into what appear to be embryonic stem cells without ever using a human embryo."[11]

That was not the only blockbuster revelation in the story. Dr. Thomson originally had "ethical concerns" about destroying human embryos for research purposes. "If human embryonic stem cell research does not make you at least a little bit uncomfortable, you have not thought about it enough," he told the *Times*.

It might have been helpful, at least for those arguing against the research on ethical and moral grounds, had he revealed that in 1998.

The research continued, as did the push for public funding. But by then embryo adoption was saving lives every day, while gains were being made with adult stem cells. And embryonic stem cells had yet to produce a single cure.

The downside? The Obama years were coming.

Those who believe in the sanctity of life and were willing to acknowledge that life begins at conception were going to miss President Bush, a Christian man who was unwilling to cave to political pressure on this important issue. This was wonderfully summarized by Tim Goeglein, the president's deputy director of the White House Office of Public Liaison. In his book *The Man in the Middle*, Goeglein noted the two White House events in 2005 and 2006 to which families who had adopted frozen embryos were invited.

These were among the most loving, caring, welcoming young parents I ever met. Their children flourished from the love and attention they received. . . . The president successfully put a human face on an otherwise abstract scientific argument about the ethics and consequences of destroying human embryos.

Short of a full ban on all federal funding, this was the most consistently pro-life decision the president could have made. It confirmed the growing view that President Bush was the most pro-life president in American history.[12]

My own family is unapologetic in its enormous gratitude for President Bush. We cannot speak for the other families in attendance at those events in the East Room of the White House, though we would be willing to bet that most, if not all, were similarly grateful. A stand on principle generally is not the currency of Washington politicians, yet President Bush spent a good deal of political capital on his defense of the sanctity of life, and we honor him for it.

The presidency of Barack Obama was not going to be so accommodating of pro-life causes, including this one. A little more than a month into his presidency, Obama signed an executive order that provided federal funding for embryonic stem cell research. Here are the key parts of the speech he gave on the subject:

Today, with the Executive Order I am about to sign, we will bring the change that so many scientists and researchers, doctors and innovators, patients and loved ones have hoped for, and fought for, these past eight years. We will lift the ban on federal funding for promising embryonic stem cell research.

At this moment, the full promise of stem cell research remains unknown, and it should not be overstated. But scientists believe these tiny cells may have the potential to help us understand, and possibly cure, some of our most devastating diseases and conditions. To regenerate a severed spinal cord and lift someone from a wheelchair. To spur insulin production and spare a child from a lifetime of needles. To treat Parkinson's, cancer, heart disease and others that affect millions of Americans and the people who love them.

But that potential will not reveal itself on its own. Medical miracles do not happen simply by accident. They result from painstaking and costly research—from years of lonely trial and error, much of which never bears fruit—and from a government willing to support that work. From life-saving vaccines, to pioneering cancer treatments, to the sequencing of the human genome—that is the story of scientific progress in America. When government fails to make these investments, opportunities are missed. Promising avenues go unexplored. Some of our best scientists leave for other countries that will sponsor their work. And those countries may surge ahead of ours in the advances that transform our lives.

But in recent years, when it comes to stem cell research, rather than furthering discovery, our government has forced what I believe is a false choice between sound science and moral values. In this case, I believe the two are not inconsistent. As a person of faith, I believe we are called to care for each other and work to ease human suffering. I believe we have been given the capacity and will to pursue this research—and the humanity and conscience to do so responsibly.[13]

I will give the first word on this matter to Hannah, ten at the time. We had always kept her apprised of the issues and explained them to her in an age-appropriate manner, so she understood the basics. She got it. She even wrote a brief letter to President Obama:

Dear President Obama,

I am Hannah Strege, the first Snowflake baby born in the United States. I am not happy with the way you are treating these Snowflakes, preborn babies. I would like you to change that. You know you are doing wrong, but if you listen to this, you could make it right. I am living proof that these Snowflake [sic] exist. We are praying that you do the right thing.

Sincerely,
Hannah Strege
Snowflake #1

Congressman Chris Smith (R-New Jersey) again provided an emphatically dissenting voice to Obama's decision. "Assertions that leftover embryos are better off dead so that their stem cells can be derived is dehumanizing and cheapens human life," he said at a news conference. "There is no such thing as leftover human life. Ask the snowflake children—cryogenically frozen embryos who were adopted—their lives are precious and priceless."[14]

He also cited Dr. Thomson's work, including Thomson's conclusion that "human embryo destroying stem cell research is not only unethical, unworkable, and unreliable, it is now demonstrably unnecessary."[15]

Dana Goldstein, writing in the progressive magazine the *American Prospect*, countered Smith's argument, beginning with the question: "But is the possibility of embryo 'adoption' really an argument against stem cell research? Not at all. There are approximately 400,000 frozen embryos in the United States, but less than 2,000 children have been born through embryo donation."[16]

Yet this notion had been debunked a few years earlier by *Chicago Tribune* columnist Steve Chapman. "Start with the claim that 400,000 frozen embryos otherwise would go to waste," he wrote. "The truth is that most of them are anything but 'surplus.' According to a 2003 survey by researchers at the RAND Corp., a California think tank, 88 percent of them are being stored for their original function: to make babies for their parents. Just 2.2 percent of the embryos have been designated for disposal and less than 3 percent for research. The latter group amounts to about 11,000 embryos."[17]

On the day after President Obama's speech, Nicholas Wade of the *New York Times* discussed the possibility that science was moving beyond research involving human embryos. "The president's support of embryonic stem cell research comes at a time when many advances have been made with other sorts of stem cells. The Japanese biologist Shinya Yamanaka found in 2007 that adult cells could be reprogrammed to an embryonic state with surprising ease. This technology 'may eventually eclipse the embryonic stem cell lines for therapeutic as well as diagnostics applications,' Dr. [Arnold] Kriegstein said. For researchers, reprogramming an adult cell can be much more convenient, and there have never been any restrictions on working with adult stem cells."[18]

❋

Every Sunday in our church, and likely in most churches in the Lutheran Church Missouri Synod, our pastor's prayers include praying for our elected officials, however we might disagree with them, asking the Lord to give them wisdom. It is always the right thing to do, of course, to pray for our leaders.

That said, it was going to be a long eight years on the pro-life front.

President Obama's next attempt to devalue human embryos came in 2012, when his administration intended to defund the Embryo Adoption Awareness Campaign, which at the time was awarding two million dollars in grants, in its 2013 fiscal budget. According to Cheryl Wetzstein in a *Washington Times* report, "The Department of Health and Human Services 'is not requesting funds for this program' because 'the Embryo Adoption program will be discontinued in FY2013,' HHS officials said in a February funding report to Congress." The HHS explained the program had "limited interest" and "a very small pool of [grant] applicants, many of whom are repeat recipients."

Wetzstein continued, "Mailee Smith, staff counsel at Americans United for Life, said such a decision is more evidence of the pro-abortion slant of this administration.

"'Why would the Obama administration cut $2 million for adoption awareness, but keep $1 million a day for Planned Parenthood?' she asked.

Smith called it "the elimination of the moral solution" to the hundreds of thousands of frozen embryos.[19]

The difficulty in introducing the concept of embryo adoption to the masses has always been problematic, which is why the Embryo Adoption Awareness Campaign was so important. Frequently we've heard about infertile couples who were unaware that embryo adoption existed until they began searching the internet to explore adoption.

"We believe that a life-affirming education program is a good thing to do," Ron Stoddart told Colorado's *Loveland Reporter-Herald*. "If there are no grants, there really is no other source of funding."[20]

Nightlight, as a result of the grants it had received, began a website called the Embryo Adoption Awareness Center that featured eight different embryo adoption programs around the country. One of the results was that couples who had completed their families and had embryos remaining discovered they had an option, one that happily allowed them to choose who received the embryos.

President Obama was unable to unilaterally eliminate the program—Congress controls the budget. But his effort did result in the outlay being cut, and the cut ran deep. "It didn't completely disappear, but we definitely felt the choke," said Daniel Nehrbass, who became the president of Nightlight Christian Adoptions when Ron Stoddart retired in 2012. "And the other agencies felt it worse. There was a peak where I think up to five agencies were receiving funds at one time. There was over a million dollars at a time being distributed, and it reached a low point of three hundred thousand dollars, and we were the only recipient one year. The criteria became more stringent and more difficult to qualify, with less money available and fewer people getting it."

Kimberly Tyson, the current director of the Snowflakes Embryo Adoption Program and the Embryo Adoption Awareness Center website, feels the sting of the cuts more acutely. "There used to be 4.2 million in the grant fund," she said. "Now it's at seven hundred thousand, and usually they award that to at least three entities. I am always praying every year, 'Lord, please know we are going to use this for your glory to help more children be born.' Our program would continue without the money, but it's great for marketing."

Obama's efforts smacked of spite. Two million dollars in the context of a federal budget is the equivalent of nickels and dimes one might find beneath their couch cushions. It is a pittance. There was no discernible reason why he could not simultaneously approve federal funding for embryonic stem cell research and also support the Embryo Adoption Awareness Campaign.

But, as he famously said regarding his election to the presidency, "I won."

No telling how many babies lost.

Proponents of federal funding of embryonic stem cell research won another victory in January of 2013 in the Supreme Court. After Obama's executive order in 2009, a lawsuit had been filed by pro-life groups, including our friend and tireless advocate Samuel B. Casey, to stop the funding on the basis that it was a violation of the Dickey-Wicker Amendment of 1996 that had banned federal funding for research on embryos. It worked its way through the courts, with some success (funding was temporarily halted in 2010 by a district court's edict) and some failure (the edict was overturned by the US Court of Appeals for the DC Circuit). Then in October, an appeal was made to the Supreme Court to take the case. The appeal was ultimately declined.

SCOTUSblog, which closely monitors and reports on all things involving the Supreme Court of the United States, posted this headline: "Stem Cell Dispute Near End?"[21]

The media, meanwhile, was relentless in its promotion of embryo-destroying research, and in the case of the far-left media, occasionally disgusting in its condemnation of those supporting embryo adoption. A writer at Jezebel, a liberal website and another creation of Gawker Media, wrote: "Who knew that 'Every Sperm Is Sacred' would be an anthem of the now-inevitable nadir of the abortion debate? Case in point: Evangelical couples doing their part to save babies by adopting . . . other couples' frozen embryos. And then unfreezing the embryos, implanting them in evangelical wombs, giving birth to them, and parading their miracle popsicle babies around as examples of how they'd been fully human this whole time."[22]

The Jezebel writer's snark did not end there. So be it. In the internet age, moral and ethical stands, or even simple disagreements, are always targets for mockery.

CHAPTER 13

Vindication

MARLENE AND I are not scientists and have never argued that embryonic stem cell research was a dead end. Our arguments against the research were based on Christian principles—that life begins at conception and that all life is precious, even that of the preborn. As Psalm 139:16 says, "Your eyes saw my unformed body; all the days ordained for me were written in your book before one of them came to be." We only knew what we knew—that destroying human embryos for research purposes was immoral and unethical as well as a dangerous step toward cloning.

But we also closely follow news on stem cell research and were aware of the progress made on ethical research using cord blood stem cells and adult stem cells that don't destroy embryos, while noting the lack of progress on embryonic stem cell research. So we have saved Hannah's cord blood.

The word *vindication* is an interesting one. Though it is not described as such, the word carries a celebratory connotation, as it does when an innocent person receives a not-guilty verdict in a court of law. We did not and do not celebrate the fact that cures had not been discovered for Parkinson's disease or diabetes or countless other debilitating diseases. The vindication in this case is simply that we and so many others in those early years—other Snowflakes families; the representatives and senators who knowledgeably and courageously stood up on behalf of "the least of these"; Dr. David Prentice, Sam Casey, and so many others who worked tirelessly behind the scenes; and Dr. Dobson, our patron saint who so generously and with complete conviction helped spread the word about embryo adoption—were on the right side of this issue. So too, to his credit, was President George W. Bush.

The first acknowledgement that President Bush was right—as far as we can recall—came from the great *Washington Post* columnist Charles Krauthammer. Krauthammer had disappointed us with his support of embryonic stem cell research in 2001, though he did so with hesitation and the caveat that the opposition arguments be treated with respect, stating that destroying embryos for research purposes "violates the categorical imperative that human life be treated as an end and not a means. It is a serious objection and should be set aside only with great trepidation."[1]

In a 2007 column with the headline "Stem Cell Vindication," Krauthammer opened by quoting James A. Thomson: "If human embryonic stem cell research does not make you at least a little bit uncomfortable, you have not thought about it enough." Noting that Thomson was the first to isolate human embryonic stem cells, Krauthammer wrote, "Last week, he (and Japan's Shinya Yamanaka) announced one of the great scientific breakthroughs since the discovery of DNA: an embryo-free way to produce genetically matched stem cells.

"The embryonic stem cell debate is over."[2]

Krauthammer went on to say this about President Bush and his stance on the research:

> The verdict is clear: Rarely has a president—so vilified for a moral stance—been so thoroughly vindicated. Why? Precisely because he took a moral stance. Precisely because, to borrow Thomson's phrase, Bush was made "a little bit uncomfortable" by the implications of embryonic experimentation. Precisely because he therefore decided that some moral line had to be drawn.
>
> In doing so, he invited unrelenting demagoguery by an

unholy trinity of Democratic politicians, research scientists, and patient advocates who insisted that anyone who would put any restriction on the destruction of human embryos could be acting only for reasons of cynical politics rooted in dogmatic religiosity—a "moral ayatollah," as Sen. Tom Harkin so scornfully put it.

Bush got it right.

Hallelujah.

Of course, news of the breakthrough did not deter embryonic stem cell research, nor did it discourage politicians from continuing to push for taxpayers funding it or President Obama from delivering on that effort.

It took another two years, in 2009, before the point made by Krauthammer was echoed through a megaphone capable of reaching a national audience—Dr. Oz on television's *The Oprah Winfrey Show*. "America's doctor," as Oprah called Dr. Mehmet Oz, was a fixture on the show, and one day he and Michael J. Fox appeared together.

Fox appeared first and noted his support for President Obama's decision to allow federal funding for embryonic stem cell research, while also stating his trust of researchers to do it ethically. Oprah then brought on Dr. Oz, vice-chair and professor of surgery at Columbia University, who caught both Oprah and Fox by surprise. The Catholic News Agency shares the narrative, beginning with Dr. Oz's bombshell:

> "Now, I'm going to say something that's going to be a bit provocative. I think, Oprah, the stem cell debate is dead, and I'll tell you why. The problem with embryonic stem cells is that embryonic stem cells come from embryos, like all of us were made from embryos. And those cells can become any cell in the body. But it's very hard to control them, and so they can become cancer."

Oprah and Fox then became visibly uncomfortable, shifting around in their chairs, as Oz explained that, contrary to Fox's earlier testimony, incredible medical advances are being made using adult stem cells and not embryonic stem cells. He claimed that, "in the last year, we've made a 10-year advancement."

Oprah responded in disbelief by saying, "In the last year we've advanced 10 years?" Oz explained, "We went places we never thought we would go."

He then boldly stated that within "single digit years" the medical community could find cures for people with not only "Parkinson's disease, but also diabetics and heart attack victims" by using adult stem cells.[3]

One would have thought everyone would have viewed this as good news—ethical research that does not destroy embryos having greater potential. One would have been wrong.

"Oprah's website summarized Oz's argument for adult stem cells with two short paragraphs, hidden 11 pages deep in a 13 page summary of the show," the Catholic News Agency reported. "Oprah.com not only avoided quoting Oz as saying 'the stem cell debate is dead,' but carefully avoided the words 'stem cell' and 'embryonic' when quoting or summarizing his remarks."[4]

Mollie Hemingway, now an editor at the *Federalist* and a Fox News contributor, noted in a story she wrote for GetReligion in 2009 that the media generally downplayed advances made by inducing pluripotent stem cells from other than embryos.

"I don't know why the media are less interested in covering these induced pluripotent stem cell advances than they have been about covering embryonic stem cell research," she wrote. "Perhaps it's because the former can't be used to inflame the culture wars. But it's terribly interesting to note the difference."[5]

Yes, it was.

Three years later, in 2012, Michael J. Fox made headlines, including this one from ABC News: "Michael J. Fox Looks Past Stem Cells in Search for Parkinson's Cure."[6]

Fox had been interviewed by Diane Sawyer, the anchor of ABC's *World News Tonight*, and though he did not specifically mention embryonic stem cell research, it was obvious that he was referring to it, given his high-profile endorsement of it as a potential cure.

"Stem cells are an avenue of research that we've pursued and continue to pursue but it's part of a broad portfolio of things that we look at," he said. "There have been some issues with stem cells, some problems along the way. . . . It's not so much that [embryonic stem cell research has] diminished in its prospects for breakthroughs as much as it's the other avenues of research have grown and multiplied and become as much or more promising. So, an answer may come from stem cell research but it's more than likely to come from another area."

Fox did not back off his support of embryonic stem cell research or his lobbying on behalf of using federal funds for it, but kudos to him for at least conceding a point for which our side routinely was criticized.

Then there was California. In 2004, its voters had passed Proposition 71, providing three billion dollars for embryonic stem cell research. In 2018, the liberal *San Francisco Chronicle* investigated whether it was money well spent. Its conclusion: probably not.

"Lofty Promises, Limited Results: After 14 Years and $3 Billion, Has California's Bet on Stem Cells Paid Off?" the headline asked. The story reported some progress, but "as thrilling as such advances are, they fall far short of what Prop. 71's promoters promised. Not a single federally approved therapy has resulted from CIRM [California Institute for Regenerative Medicine]-funded science. The predicted financial windfall has not materialized. The bulk of CIRM grants have gone to basic research, training programs and building new laboratories, not to clinical trials testing the kinds of potential cures and therapies the billions of dollars were supposed to deliver."[7]

So, what has been the response? This headline in the *National Review* sums it up succinctly: "California Stem-Cell Agency Wants More Voter Money."[8] So does this excerpt from an NPR story: "Backers of stem cell research plan to ask voters in the state to pony up for round two. The projected ask this time: $5 billion, in a measure the backers hope to place on the California ballot in 2020."[9]

It never ends.

CHAPTER 14

God's Gifts

THE YEAR 2017 was a memorable one for us and a time of transition for Hannah. She graduated from high school and would soon be heading off to Biola University in La Mirada, California. That year also marked the twentieth anniversary of the founding of the Snowflakes Embryo Adoption Program. To celebrate the occasion, Nightlight Christian Adoptions' Loveland, Colorado, office hosted a picnic for Snowflake families at Fairgrounds Park. Families came from around the country.

Hannah, then eighteen, was among those asked to speak, and her brief speech included this:

> Your story, our stories, are unique and long, but they make people listen. God certainly had a plan for all of us back in 1997, and I am so proud to say that over five hundred [Snowflake] babies have been born since. And I couldn't be more amazed at the God who orchestrated this all for a purpose.
>
> I am very comfortable with my story, and I share it openly for anyone who wants to listen. It is also a great way to share the gospel of Jesus and bring it back to the meaning of life.
>
> I recently did my senior project on family, and the struggle between figuring out who my parents really are. My thesis was this: "St. Paul of Tarsus often used adoption as a metaphor for the gospel of Jesus Christ. The similarities between earthly adoption and God's loving adoption of us as sons and

daughters are obvious. Although both concepts are so simple a child can understand, they both carry such incredible emotional weight that they take a lifetime to work out and understand." I came to the conclusion that one family holds my biology and the other holds my heart, and now I just have one big extended family.

John 14:18 says, "I will not leave you as orphans; I will come to you." That is exactly it. God came to us and placed us in our forever homes. The Bible says that God works good for those who love him. And Nightlight is built on that legacy.

It was a proud moment for Marlene and me. And it was admirable that Hannah acknowledged the story was not hers alone. Every family that has adopted frozen embryos, as well as those who have placed frozen embryos for adoption, deserves to take a bow. Dr. James Dobson, in a letter to Nightlight commemorating the occasion, noted as such.

Dear Snowflakes Families,

I am so pleased to join you in celebrating the 20th anniversary of the Snowflakes Embryo Adoption Program.

I still recall vividly the phone call I had with Marlene and John Strege back in 1997. After seeking counsel from professionals in the medical community, I told Marlene and John that I believed embryo adoption would be honorable before God. They have become great friends with whom, even to this day, I continue to keep in touch. Their daughter, Hannah, has become such a delightful young lady.

Our God is the Creator and Sustainer of life and each of you have determined to honor God by either placing or adopting embryos to give them life!

Today I would like to applaud the placing parents for choosing to donate embryos for reproduction, thus giving them an opportunity to be born and live the life for which God created them. I applaud the adopting families for choosing this very unique and special adoption path for bringing children into your lives.

Over 500 babies! Isn't that fantastic? It is my prayer that more families like yours will choose life and encourage others to do the same.

Congratulations,
James Dobson, PhD
Founder & President
Family Talk

Hannah found herself the center of attention among many of the younger Snowflake children in attendance at the picnic. Though Hannah does not seek such attention and often is uncomfortable with it, she understands it and was great with those kids. She met Amelia, the daughter of Heather and Jason Mayer, a wonderful Christian couple from Washington State who had adopted several frozen embryos. The girls had previously exchanged emails discussing their American Girl dolls. (Several months after the picnic, in an interesting turn, the Mayers learned via DNA kits that Amelia was not among the embryos transferred; she was in fact their biological daughter.)

Hannah also got reacquainted—to the extent they were ever acquainted, having met when they were toddlers—with Snowflakes number two and three, twins Mark and Luke Borden.

The Snowflake children there ranged in age from one to eighteen, and from Snowflake number one, Hannah, to Snowflake number four hundred seventy, Marley Wilson. One of the best moments of the picnic occurred when Hannah held Marley, who had spent nearly eighteen years as a frozen embryo before her parents, Elizabeth and Marty Wilson, adopted her. Hannah and Marley each had been consigned to a frozen orphanage close to the same time, yet one was an adult and one was a toddler—miracles, both of them.

Everyone's embryo adoption story, like the Snowflakes themselves, is unique, no two alike, but all contain a common denominator: God in their midst.

"Marley is perfect in every way," Elizabeth told BabyCenter.com. "Marley was created and saved for us before my husband and I even met, and before I even knew I would want children one day. It shows God has the perfect plan."[1]

We have been privileged to know many of these remarkable families, fellow pro-life Christians who prayerfully and selflessly—and perhaps apprehensively too—chose embryo adoption, as uncertain as they were on how it might play out. Each of them also advanced the cause by defending the sanctity of human life and honoring God in the process.

Debbie and Brian Struiksma's story illustrates this perfectly. Debbie had premature ovarian failure and learned about embryo adoption via a coworker who had heard Marlene discussing it with Dr. Dobson on his radio show. She went to see a fertility doctor, who highly recommended using donated eggs. She informed him she was interested in embryo adoption. He dismissed the idea out of hand, instead saying he could find embryos through his clinic. "He looked me square in the face and said, 'God took away your eggs, but I will give you a baby,'" Debbie said.

This was the wrong thing to say to this strong, passionate Christian woman.

"The look on my face must have been priceless, because as he was talking, I was having my own conversation with God. It went something like, 'God, did you just hear what he said?' . . . I could not get out of that office fast enough." She soon found a supportive doctor, and she and Brian were matched with two genetic families. They became the parents of sixteen embryos, went through three embryo transfers, and have two beautiful children born three years apart. "Luke and Noel are not genetically connected to each other or to us," Debbie said, "but God knit us together before the beginning of time. He *always* has a plan."

Two pastors of Lutheran Church Missouri Synod churches and their wives went through the Snowflakes program and adopted frozen embryos. Pastor Tim Lawson and his wife, Ruth, had hoped to start their family shortly after they were married, but it was not happening, and they discovered that having a family was likely to happen only via adoption. But Ruth, listening to a Focus on the Family broadcast one day, learned about Snowflakes Embryo Adoption. "How amazing—the thought of carrying your adoptive child!" she said. She and Tim adopted three embryos, but the transfer was unsuccessful.

So they changed course and chose traditional adoption, and seven months later their son Micah James was born. They returned to embryo adoption and were blessed with Shiloh Ethan, Snowflake baby number three hundred eighty-three. They had their third child, Emery Mae, via a traditional adoption. "You know the phrase, 'When you tell God your plans, he laughs'?" she asked. "Well, that was most definitely true for Tim and me." On a date one night, they both agreed their family was complete. They were in for a surprise. "Eight months later, we welcomed Noelle Ann into our family. The Lord most certainly knitted our family together in miraculous ways, and Tim and I are honored to be chosen as our precious children's parents."

Pastor Luke Timm and his wife, Joni, already had three children and were discussing having one more. They frequently had discussed adoption, and it was their desire, and ultimately their calling, Luke said, to assist those in distress—either a single mother or a couple unable to raise their child. Once they learned of embryo adoption, they decided this would be the path they'd take. They were matched with a couple from Alaska who had four frozen embryos remaining.

The Timms adopted the four remaining embryos, though only two survived the thawing. They transferred the surviving two and were assured that, given the age of the embryos, it was unlikely for either of them to split. "We had a 33 percent chance of having twins, a 66 percent chance of a singleton, and 0 percent chance of having any more than two," Pastor Timm said. When the couple eventually went in for an ultrasound, they discovered they were having triplets—the Timmlets, as they were called when they arrived via C-section a few months later— happily doubling the Timms' number of children.

The passion of those who have adopted embryos cannot be overstated. They are spirited and driven by the spiritual. Meet Doni and Jim Brinkman, parents of Tanner, Snowflake baby number eight, and three other children via domestic adoption. Doni's passion was evident in a beautifully written testimonial she shared with me, which was presented to Australia's Senate Committee in 2002 regarding its Inquiry into Research Involving Embryos and Prohibition of Human Cloning Bill. She wrote in part:

> It is because of Tanner and his siblings that I submit this testimony. As a mother privileged enough to carry my adopted children, I know first-hand what a miracle life is and how precious that life is, even while in its tiniest embryonic stages. . . .
>
> My goal is simply this, that you will be left in awe at the miracle of life, the beauty of adoption, and the incredible gift of children, even in their tiniest form—and that you would be encouraged to support an act that would protect and respect what is most precious and treasured, our little ones and ourselves.

Courtney and Tim Atnip's story is a reminder that the ultimate authority is God, not people, even people with medical degrees. At thirty, Courtney had received a diagnosis of premature ovarian failure. After a period of mourning and reevaluating how they wished to grow their family, Courtney still wanted to experience pregnancy. In the meantime, Tim's aunt had listened to an episode of Dr. Dobson's radio show, presumably one featuring Marlene and Hannah. She told the Atnips about it, and they decided on embryo adoption. After going through the requisite steps, they were matched with a family with eleven frozen embryos.

When their fertility doctor received the embryos, he examined them and told the Atnips that the quality of the embryos was insufficient and unlikely to result in a pregnancy. They requested the doctor move forward with the transfer regardless of his concern about their quality. "He told us not to expect a positive pregnancy result," she said. "We politely told him he's not God and that we were covered in prayer, so no matter the outcome, we were at peace. I believe statistics are important simply to keep perspective. But I also believe that God doesn't care too much about statistics. . . . Statistically, Carter shouldn't be here. But he is."

The Atnips then adopted a baby from China, Abby. And when Courtney was forty, notwithstanding a ten-year-old diagnosis of premature ovarian failure, she became pregnant with Paisley.

Dave and Kelly Keim's experience was described by then Congressman Mike Pence (R-Indiana) on the floor of the House of Representatives in 2004. "They are in town today to stand with many others in this building to oppose embryonic stem cell research," Pence said, speaking of the Snowflakes contingent's lobbying politician.

> Why would people come [here] from Berne, Indiana? The answer can be found in their 18-month-old twins, Caroline and Spencer, who are a daily and profound reminder that embryonic adoption should be preferred in the law always over destroying human embryos for stem cell research.
>
> Mr. Speaker, Caroline and Spencer Keim are fully human today, just as they were 18 short months ago when they were in the frozen embryonic stage of their development. They stand as a living testament to the truth that it would have been

morally wrong to destroy their embryonic lives, even for well-intentioned medical research.[2]

Heather and Doug Hutchens of Guthrie, Oklahoma, also were among those who traveled to Washington, DC—twice, in fact—to defend the sanctity of human life and to remind the politicians in favor of embryo-destroying stem cell research that an embryo is life itself. They have three sons, all of them adopted as frozen embryos—"God's perfect plan," they call it—to prove the point. Their identical twins, Sam and Ben, are now eighteen-year-old honor students and freshmen at Oklahoma State University, interested in studying sports media; David, fifteen, is a high-school sophomore with myriad interests.

Two families with ordinary American surnames, Murray and Johnson, are not ordinary in any manner. Suzanne and Peter Murray were finally diagnosed with infertility issues ten years into their marriage. The Murrays, staunchly pro-life Catholics who have lobbied the Catholic Church to embrace embryo adoption, opted to start their family that way, resulting in daughter Mary Elizabeth, born in 2003. Two years later they hosted sisters Anya, twelve, and Galina, six, part of a group of Russian orphans Nightlight Christian Adoptions brought to the United States to stay with host families for two weeks. Suzanne and Peter fell in love with them and adopted them. Then they returned to embryo adoption, resulting in a fourth child, a boy named P. J.

Then there are Pennsylvanians Kate and Steve Johnson and daughter Zara. They were among those in attendance in the East Room of the White House in 2005 when President Bush reiterated his stand against federal funding of embryonic stem cell research. Anne Morse wrote about them in *National Review*.

"Among the parents was Steve Johnson, a paraplegic who, with his wife Kate, adopted an embryo whom they named Zara—now a little girl in a pink flowered dress and blond curls playing near her father's wheelchair," she wrote. "Johnson described the years of pain, high medical costs, and limited mobility he'd endured after a bike accident 12 years before. 'My soul aches for a cure for my paralysis,' he said—but not at the cost of a child's life. 'Would I kill my daughter so I could walk again? Of course not. Then why do we think it is okay to kill someone else's kid?' he asked."[3]

Tragically, Steve was later killed when he was hit by a speeding ambulance, but he deserves to be remembered and honored for his selfless commitment to others.

These families—with the exceptions of the pastors and their wives, who came to embryo adoption later—were among those involved in one or more of the trips we made to Washington, DC, to lobby representatives and senators, to raise media awareness of the cause of embryo adoption and against embryo-destroying research, and to help influence an important policy decision at the highest levels of government. All of them returned to their hometowns and courageously shared their stories with local media—reaching out at the grass-roots level to introduce others to embryo adoption. We honor and appreciate all of them, both those mentioned here and those not mentioned.

It is important to remember that the story does not end here. The number of babies born via embryo adoption has continued to grow significantly and will continue to do so as greater numbers learn of the option. Collectively, these adopted frozen embryos who have been given a chance at life, and those to follow, will help make the world a better place. The first three Snowflake babies are already pursuing fields that will put them in positions to make important contributions to society. Hannah is a sociology major who feels called to enter social work generally and the adoption field specifically. Luke Borden joined the Marine Corps, and his twin brother Mark has joined the Coast Guard.

"We have different gifts, according to the grace given to each of us," the twelfth chapter of Romans says. "If your gift is prophesying, then prophesy in accordance with your faith; if it is serving, then serve; if it is teaching, then teach; if it is to encourage, then give encouragement; if it is giving, then give generously; if it is to lead, do it diligently; if it is to show mercy, do it cheerfully" (vv. 6–8).

Every one of the previously frozen embryos, those already born and those to come, will find their own way, make their own contribution. God has the road map, and the first step is the most important one. The first step is trust. Proverbs 3:5, "Trust in the Lord with all your heart and lean not on your own understanding," is such an instructive Bible verse, a reminder that as much as we like to think we can script our futures, we can't—God is in control. We walk by faith, the Bible tells us, not by sight.

Our own story reflects the truth of that wisdom. Marlene once told Ron Stoddart that when we wanted to adopt frozen embryos, we proceeded prayerfully but *blindly*, unsure where this was going but choosing to trust in the Lord, to walk by faith. Having done so, we were blessed beyond all measure.

We were blessed with a Snowflake named Hannah.

Epilogue

On a warm August day in 2001, in the studio at Focus on the Family in Colorado Springs, Colorado, Dr. Dobson asked Hannah to sing him a song during a recording of his radio show. She sweetly sang "Jesus Loves the Little Children," not only for him but also for millions of listeners around the country and the world. Among those listeners was Mitzi, a wonderful, kind, fun, and faithful Christian woman. A few years later, I had the idea that we should ask parents of Snowflake babies if they might write letters to Hannah, so that one day she would understand the impact she had had. Mitzi and her husband, Jack, who since have become dear friends, were among those who wrote to Hannah. Their letter, reproduced here with their permission, was a beautiful, loving testament to how God was working in all our lives.

Dear Hannah,

A few years ago, when I was driving home from work late at night, I turned on the radio to listen to Dr. Dobson's broadcast. A little girl caught my attention, because she was singing and sounded sooo cute! I continued to listen as Dr. Dobson introduced that little girl as Hannah, and he went on to tell your story about how you were adopted.

As I was listening, I just knew that Jack and I were supposed to adopt embryos! Just like your Mom and Dad, my husband and I were unable to have children, and we had always considered adoption, but didn't really know where to start. After hearing you sing and talk on the radio, I was so excited, and I called Nightlight the very next day for the paperwork to start the adoption process.

It took about two years for our embryos to come, but worth the wait! We had 3 embryos put inside of me, and two of them "took." I was pregnant with twins! Little Chase and Dakota were born on September 4th, 2004. They are a miracle to me, and so are you! Actually, I refer to you as my angel. If I had not heard you on the radio, I might not have these two beautiful boys.

Thank you for being so brave and involved in the embryo program. You have helped so many people, and are such a great example of God's love.

We love you!

Jack and Mitzi

God was using Hannah, though at the time she was too young to know that, and we did not yet entirely know the extent of her impact either. Apple cofounder Steve Jobs, in a commencement speech he gave at Stanford University on June 14, 2005, spoke about connecting the dots. He noted how he had dropped out of college and then taken a calligraphy class by chance. In the class, he learned about typefaces, which eventually influenced his decision to include them in the first Macintosh computer.

If I had never dropped out, I would have never dropped in on this calligraphy class, and personal computers might not have the wonderful typography that they do. Of course, it was impossible to connect the dots looking forward when I was in college. But it was very, very clear looking backward 10 years later.

Again, you can't connect the dots looking forward; you

can only connect them looking backward. So you have to trust
that the dots will somehow connect in your future. You have to
trust in something—your gut, destiny, life, karma, whatever.[1]

We trusted in the Lord, but to Jobs's point, only in hindsight were
we able to see the totality of God at work in our lives, to see how "the
dots connected." In our case, the dots were a series of events that had to
occur for us to have Hannah and that God used to his glory to start the
Snowflakes Embryo Adoption Program.

The word *snowflakes*, incidentally, has become a generic description
of adopted frozen embryos, notwithstanding that in the context of
the Snowflakes Embryo Adoption Program, the word is a registered
trademark. Look up "snowflake children" on Wikipedia and the entry
begins, "Snowflake children is a term used by organizations that promote the adoption of frozen embryos."[2]

Snowflakes has turned up in a variety of unusual places. For
instance, Emily Giffin, a prolific best-selling author of fiction, mentions
Snowflakes in her novel *Baby Proof*, published in 2006. In one scene,
the character Daphne says, "We're also looking into this really cool program called Snowflake. Have you heard of it?"

Daphne's friend mentions that it's controversial, "I guess because
these parents essentially believe that the embryos are children. Which
is why they call it 'adoption' and not 'donation.'"

Daphne nonetheless concludes that it's "a great option."[3]

There, too, is the novel *Snowflakes*, published in 2016 by Michael
L. Rea, one of Hannah's favorite teachers at Rancho Christian High
School in Temecula, California. His dedication reads, "In appreciation
of Hannah S., who first introduced me to the story of the Snowflake
Babies and who provided the inspiration and opened my mind to the
possibility."[4]

But the most prominent place we've seen Snowflakes turn up is in
President George W. Bush's book *Decision Points*. He wrote an entire

chapter on stem cells, the research, and his opposition to providing federal funds for embryonic stem cell research. He noted a meeting he had with representatives of National Right to Life in July 2001. "They opposed any research that destroyed embryos," President Bush wrote. They explained why, noting that these stem cell clusters "had the potential to grow into a person," and that all of us had started that way. "As evidence," he wrote, "they pointed to a new program run by Nightlight Christian Adoptions. The agency secured permission from IVF participants to place their unused frozen embryos up for adoption. Loving mothers had the embryos implanted in them and carried the babies— known as snowflakes—to term. The message was unmistakable: Within every frozen embryo were the beginnings of a child."[5]

He also mentioned "snowflake babies" in recalling the first veto of his presidency. It was no surprise that on January 15, 2008, in advance of Nightlight Christian Adoptions' annual dinner, the agency received the following letter from the White House:

> I send greetings to those gathered for the 10th Annual Gala Dinner of Nightlight Christian Adoptions.
>
> Few missions in life are more rewarding than uniting children with loving, supportive, and caring parents. Since 1997, NCA's Snowflakes Frozen Embryo Adoption Program has connected donating and adoptive families, resulting to date in the birth of more than 150 children. These children are living reminders that adoptions are stories of celebration, hope, and love. This event is an opportunity to recognize the parents and youth who have found the gift of one another and to honor those dedicated to respecting life in all stages.
>
> My Administration remains committed to the steadfast belief in the dignity and the promise of every life, and we are encouraging more citizens to choose adoptions. I appreciate NCA and all those who are working to make America a more

just and welcoming place. I also commend parents who have
shared their homes and hearts with children in need. Your
compassionate efforts help shape lives and demonstrate the
great character of our Nation.

Laura and I send our best wishes for a memorable event.

George Bush

This would have been inconceivable to us as our story was unfolding,
as was the manner in which Snowflake babies became a powerful pro-
life instrument in the embryonic stem cell research debate, the start of
which coincided with the birth of Hannah.

Coincided. The renowned pastor Greg Laurie wrote in the website
WND, "A unique feature of the book of Esther is that the name of God
is never specifically mentioned in it. However, God is present in this
book from beginning to end, just as He is present in every scene and
in every movement of every event. It reminds us that for the Christian,
there is no coincidence in our lives, just providence."[6]

We never could have foreseen all that occurred from our simple
desire to have a baby. "It was one of those things that you say, 'That's
not a coincidence,'" Ron Stoddart said to me on a visit to Loveland,
Colorado. "There is no way that any of us was smart enough to have
orchestrated that. It was all building blocks." He, too, cited the biblical
example of Esther and how "he has put you there for a time such as
this." He noted what so many of us go through in life, that there are
"things that God prepares for you, and you think, Why?"

Tim Tebow, a Heisman Trophy winner and a devout Christian, provided a great example. Tebow always posted a Bible verse reference on
his eye black. For the University of Florida's national championship
game with Oklahoma in 2009, he wrestled with what verse to use and
said that God had moved him to use John 3:16—"the essence of our
Christianity" and "the essence of our hope," he said.

For God so loved the world, that he gave his only begotten Son, that whosoever believeth in him should not perish, but have everlasting life. (KJV)

Reportedly, there were ninety-four million internet searches of John 3:16. Ninety-four million.

"Honestly my first thought was, 'How do ninety-four million people not know John 3:16?'" Tebow said. "I was just so humbled by how big the God is that we serve."[7]

Marlene noted God working in our lives when she was a guest on Dr. Dobson's radio show in August of 2005. The topic was how Bill Frist, the Senate majority leader at the time, had abandoned his otherwise steadfast pro-life positions by declaring his support of federally funding embryo-destroying stem cell research, and how President Bush steadfastly opposed doing so and backed up his stance with a veto.

"Looking back now," Marlene said on the radio show, "I totally see the hand of God, that God's plan was well underway for these embryos, a plan of adoption rather than destruction."[8]

We all begin our journeys armed with vivid blueprints of how it all will play out. Yet over time, what unfolds is a series of what seem to be random events—hopefully more of them pleasant than unpleasant—that, stitched together, form a quilt that tells the story of our lives. The pattern and the purpose, known clearly to God, are rarely so apparent to us at first. When life isn't unfolding according to our plans, we tend to ask God why.

We were guilty of this, too, until we began to see how the dots were connecting, how this seemingly random series of events was not random at all: Marlene's babysitting job in the seventies that brought Ron Stoddart into our lives. Infertility. Dr. Dobson, prohibitive odds notwithstanding, phoning Marlene and embracing our cause. The creation of the Snowflakes Embryo Adoption Program. The birth of Hannah. How her birth coincided with the discovery of embryo-destroying research. Dr. Dobson's using his God-given platform to spread the word on embryo adoption and to campaign against the immorality of the research. Marlene's testifying in Congress. A presidential veto. Thousands, even tens of thousands, of frozen embryos saved from destruction. And finally, what all of this represents in its totality: a collective stand on behalf of the sanctity of human life that honors the biblical edict to speak for those who cannot speak for themselves.

Finally, it all made sense.

"For I know the plans I have for you," the Lord declared in Jeremiah. All glory to God, for how our lives have played out surely was not coincidence. It was providence.

Notes

Introduction

1. "President Discusses Stem Cell Research Policy," The White House, July 19, 2006, https://georgewbush-whitehouse.archives.gov/news/releases/2006/07/text/20060719-3.html#.
2. Rick Warren, "Day 13," *Rick Warren's Daily Devotional,* accessed October 2, 2019, https://www.bible.com/reading-plans/135-rick-warrens-daily-devotional/day/13.

Chapter 1: What Would God Think?

1. James Dobson, *Solid Answers* (Carol Stream, IL: Tyndale, 1997), 499.
2. Dobson, *Solid Answers,* 497–99.

Chapter 3: Snowflakes

1. James Dobson, *When God Doesn't Make Sense* (Carol Stream, IL: Tyndale, 1993), 58–59.

Chapter 5: Hannah's First Radio Show

1. All quotes from this interview are from the author's transcription of the recorded broadcast, supplied to the author on CD by Focus on the Family. The interview was recorded May 26, 1999, and the show aired in July 1999 by Focus on the Family Broadcast.

Chapter 6: The Great Debate

1. "Thomson Lab," Morgridge Institute for Research, accessed December 4, 2019, https://morgridge.org/research/regenerative-biology/thomson-lab/.

2. Gretchen Vogel, "Capturing the Promise of Youth," *Science* 286, no. 5448 (December 17, 1999): 2238, https://science.sciencemag.org/content/286/5448/2238.summary.

3. Pope John Paul II, *Evangelium Vitae*, Libreria Editrice Vaticana, March 25, 1995, http://w2.vatican.va/content/john-paul-ii/en/encyclicals/documents/hf_jp-ii_enc_25031995_evangelium-vitae.html.

4. Michael Kinsley, as quoted in George Weigel, "Stem Cells and the Logic of the Nazis," *Los Angeles Times*, September 3, 2000, https://www.latimes.com/archives/la-xpm-2000-sep-03-op-14832-story.html.

5. Weigel, "Stem Cells and the Logic of the Nazis."

6. Russell Saltzman, "Mary Tyler Moore's Autograph and What I Did with It," *Touchstone*, June 2001, https://www.touchstonemag.com/archives/article.php?id=14-05-013-v.

7. All quotes from this subcommittee hearing are taken from the transcript for Senate Hearing 106-413, "Stem Cell Research, Part 3," accessed December 4, 2019, https://www.govinfo.gov/content/pkg/CHRG-106shrg66482/html/CHRG-106shrg66482.htm.

Chapter 7: Hannah Goes to Washington

1. Megan Kearl, "Nightlight Christian Adoptions, et al. v. Thompson, et al. (2001)," *Embryo Project Encyclopedia*, September 28, 2010, https://embryo.asu.edu/pages/nightlight-christian-adoptions-et-al-v-thompson-et-al-2001.

2. Charles Krauthammer, "Life in the Balance," *Washington Post*, June 29, 2001, https://www.washingtonpost.com/archive/opinions/2001/06/29/life-in-the-balance/af8a3e7e-75ee-457a-a91f-b357cc3e7238/.

3. Krauthammer, "Life in the Balance."

4. All quotes from this subcommittee hearing are taken from the transcript for "Opportunities and Advancements in Stem Cell

Research," ser. no. 107-38, House of Representatives 107th Congress First Session, July 17, 2001, https://www.govinfo.gov/content/pkg/CHRG-107hhrg77248/html/CHRG-107hhrg77248.htm.

5. Steve Chapman, "The Benefits of Stem Cell Research—and the Costs," *Chicago Tribune*, July 15, 2001, https://www.chicagotribune.com/news/ct-xpm-2001-07-15-0107150406-story.html.

6. Chapman, "The Benefits of Stem Cell Research."

7. "Remarks by President Bush and His Holiness Pope John Paul II," The White House, July 23, 2001, https://georgewbush-whitehouse.archives.gov/news/releases/2001/07/20010723-1.html.

8. "Transcript: Bush, Berlusconi News Conference," CNN.com, July 23, 2001, http://www.cnn.com/2001/WORLD/europe/07/23/bush.berlusconi.transcript/.

Chapter 8: President Bush Makes the Call

1. All quotes from this interview are from the author's transcription of the recorded broadcast, supplied to the author on CD by Focus on the Family. The show was aired August 9, 2001, by Focus on the Family Broadcast.

2. All quotes of the president in this address are taken from the transcript "President Discusses Stem Cell Research," The White House, August 9, 2001, https://georgewbush-whitehouse.archives.gov/news/releases/2001/08/text/20010809-2.html.

3. All quotes by Dr. Dobson and Dr. Walter Larimore in this section are from the author's transcription of the recorded broadcast, supplied to the author on CD by Focus on the Family. The show was aired August 9, 2001, by Focus on the Family Broadcast.

4. Jeffrey Kluger and Michael D. Lemonick, "And What About the Science?," *Time*, August 20, 2001, http://content.time.com/time/magazine/article/0,9171,1000564,00.html.

5. *Time*, cover, August 20, 2001, https://time.com/vault/year/2001/.

Chapter 9: The Battle Continues

1. Marcus Baram, "Horton's Who: The Unborn?," ABC News, March 17, 2008.
2. Andrew Bair, "15 of the Greatest Pro-Life Quotes of All Time," LifeNews.com, September 3, 2013, https://www.lifenews.com /2013/09/03/15-of-the-greatest-pro-life-quotes-of-all-time/.
3. Ron Stoddart, "Frozen Embryos: Biotech's Hidden Dilemma," *Christianity Today*, July 28, 2010, https://www.christianitytoday .com/ct/2010/july/25.46.html.
4. Program Announcement No. 2002-01, 67 Fed. Reg. 48655 (July 25, 2002), https://www.govinfo.gov/content/pkg/FR-2002-07-25 /pdf/02-18826.pdf.
5. Ronald Bailey, "Federal Embryo Adoption," *Reason*, March 27, 2002, https://reason.com/2002/03/27/federal-embryo-adoption/.
6. Laura Meckler (Associated Press), "Stem-Cell Fight Shifts to Embryo Adoption," *Seattle Times*, August 21, 2002, http://com munity.seattletimes.nwsource.com/archive/?date=20020821 &slug=embryos210.
7. Meckler, "Stem-Cell Fight."
8. Kathryn Miehl, "Pre Embryos: The Tiniest Speck of Potential Life Carrying the Seeds for Sweeping Change," *Journal of Technology Law and Policy* 4, no. 3 (Fall 2003): 32, https://tlp.law.pitt.edu/ojs /index.php/tlp/article/download/12/12.
9. Meckler, "Stem-Cell Fight."
10. Wesley J. Smith, "Media Bias on Adult Stem Cell Research Contin- ues," *National Review*, April 23, 2002, reprinted by permission in LifeIssues.net, accessed December 4, 2019, http://www.lifeissues .net/writers/smit/smit_09mediabias.html.
11. Excerpt from a copy of the letter provided to the author by the Subcommittee on Criminal Justice, Drug Policy, and Human Resources, Committee on Government Reform, US House of Representatives.

12. Nigel M. de S. Cameron and Jennifer Lahl, "Legislating Medicine/ California's Bizarre Cloning Proposition," *San Francisco Chronicle*, July 11, 2002, https://www.sfgate.com/opinion/openforum /article/Legislating-Medicine-California-s-bizarre-2708566 .php.

13. Megan Garvey, "State Bets on the Promise of Stem Cell Research," *Los Angeles Times*, November 4, 2004, https://www.latimes.com /archives/la-xpm-2004-nov-04-me-stemcell4-story.html.

Chapter 10: DC Lobbyists

1. Sarah Blustain, "Embryo Adoption," *New York Times Magazine*, December 11, 2005, https://www.nytimes.com/2005/12/11/mag azine/embryo-adoption.html.

2. *Merriam-Webster*, s.v. "scare quotes," accessed December 4, 2019, https://www.merriam-webster.com/dictionary/scare%20quotes.

3. Chris Emery, "Embryo Adoption Generates Children—and Critics," Capital News Service, March 30, 2006, https://cnsmary land.org/cns/wire/2006-editions/03-March-editions/060330 -Thursday/EmbryoAdoption_CNS-UMCP.html.

4. Stem Cell Research Enhancement Act of 2004, H.R. 4682, 108th Cong. (2004), https://www.congress.gov/bill/108th-con gress/house-bill/4682/text.

5. "Ron Reagan: Text of Tuesday Speech," *Houston Chronicle*, July 27, 2004, https://www.chron.com/news/politics/amp/Ron -Reagan-Text-of-Tuesday-speech-1508780.php.

6. *San Diego Union-Tribune*, August 11, 2004, as quoted in "Barbara Boxer on Abortion," On the Issues, accessed December 4, 2019, http://www.issues2000.org/Social/Barbara_Boxer_Abortion.htm.

7. Jodi Wilgoren, "Kerry Takes On Bush over Stance on Stem-Cell Research," *New York Times*, October 5, 2004, https://www.ny times.com/2004/10/05/politics/campaign/kerry-takes-on-bush -over-stance-on-stemcell-research.html.

8. All quotes of the president in this address are taken from the transcript "Remarks on Bioethics," Public Papers of the Presidents of the United States: George W. Bush (2005, Book I), May 24, 2005, https://www.govinfo.gov/content/pkg/PPP-2005-book1/html /PPP-2005-book1-doc-pg868.htm.

9. Laurie Kellman (Associated Press), "Mrs. Reagan Likely to Push Stem Cell Bill," Fox News, June 17, 2005, https://www.foxnews .com/story/mrs-reagan-likely-to-push-stem-cell-bill.

10. 151 Cong. Rec. S9323 (daily ed. July 29, 2005), https://www .congress.gov/crec/2005/07/29/CREC-2005-07-29-senate.pdf.

11. Joel Roberts, "Frist Backs Stem Cell Research," CBS News, July 29, 2005, https://www.cbsnews.com/news/frist-backs-stem-cell -research/.

12. James Dobson in a Focus on the Family press release, as quoted in "Perkins, Dobson Go After Frist," Uncommon Sense (blog), July 29, 2005, http://ucsense.blogspot.com/2005/07/perkins-dobson -go-after-frist.html.

13. All quotes by Claude Allen and Marlene in this section are from the author's transcription of the recorded broadcast, supplied to the author on CD by Focus on the Family. The show was aired August 4, 2005, by Focus on the Family Broadcast.

14. "CSI Pushes Abortion Agenda," Catholic League for Religious and Civil Rights, December 12, 2005, https://www.catholicleague .org/csi-pushes-abortion-agenda/.

15. "CSI Pushes Abortion Agenda," Catholic League for Religious and Civil Rights.

Chapter 11: Thank You, Mr. President

1. From 4CBS Denver, as quoted in Jeralyn Merritt, "President Bush Disses Diana DeGette," 5280, July 12, 2006, https://www.5280 .com/2006/07/president-bush-disses-diana-degette/.

2. John Farrell, "Rove Predicts Bush's 1st Veto," Denver Post, July

10, 2006, https://www.denverpost.com/2006/07/10rove-predicts
-bushs-1st-veto/.

3. All quotes from Senator Brownback's presentation taken from 152
Cong. Rec. S7591–92 (daily ed. July 17, 2006), https://congress
.gov/109/crec/2006/07/17/CREC-2006-07-17.pdf. See also the C-
SPAN 2 video of Brownback in the July 17, 2006, Senate debate,
accessed December 4, 2019, http://images1.americanprogress.org
/il80web20037/ThinkProgress/2006/brownbackhannah.320.240
.mov.

4. Dana Milbank, "Stem Cell Debate Wedges Bush Between a
Rock and a Hard Place," *Washington Post*, July 18, 2006, https://
www.washingtonpost.com/archive/politics/2006/07/18/stem-cell
-debate-wedges-bush-between-a-rock-and-a-hard-place/280de7ce
-3b7e-4505-9f66-09e8df3928bd/?utm_term=.d09a8d4c6fa6.

5. Margaret Carlson, "Bush Snubs Science in Deference to Snowflakes," *HuffPost*, July 20, 2006, https://www.huffpost.com/entry
/bush-snubs-science-in-def_1_b_25452.

6. "Message to the House of Representatives," The White House,
July 19, 2006, https://georgewbush-whitehouse.archives.gov/news
/releases/2006/07/20060719-5.html.

7. "Bush's Veto Message," *New York Times*, July 19, 2006, https://
www.nytimes.com/2006/07/19/washington/text-stem.html.

8. Joni Eareckson Tada, "The Threat of Biotech," *Christianity Today*,
March 1, 2003, https://www.christianitytoday.com/ct/2003/march
/8.60.html.

9. "President Discusses Stem Cell Research Policy," The White
House, July 19, 2006, https://georgewbush-whitehouse.archives
.gov/news/releases/2006/07/20060719-3.html.

10. "Joni Eareckson Tada, a Quadriplegic, Supports President Bush's
Veto on Embryonic Stem Cell Bill," *Breaking Christian News*,
July 21, 2006, https://www.breakingchristiannews.com/articles
/display_art.html?ID=2788.

11. "Stem Cell Research Enhancement Act of 2005—Veto Message from the President of the United States (H. Doc. no. 109-127)," *Congressional Record*, July 19, 2006, https://www.congress.gov /congressional-record/2006/7/19/house-section/article/h5435-1.

12. "Nightlight Christian Adoptions, Snowflakes Mentioned in President Bush's 'Decision Points,'" Nightlight, accessed December 4, 2019, https://www.nightlight.org/2011/01/nightlight-christian -adoptions-snowflakes-mentioned-in-president-bushs-decision -points/.

13. Alex Pareene, "How About 'Li'l Freezies'?," *Wonkette*, July 18, 2006, https://www.wonkette.com/how-about-lil-freezies-2569504520 .amp.html.

14. Liza Mundy, "Souls on Ice: America's Embryo Glut and the Wasted Promise of Stem Cell Research," *Mother Jones*, June/July 2006, https://www.motherjones.com/politics/2006/07/souls-ice -americas-embryo-glut-and-wasted-promise-stem-cell-research/.

Chapter 12: Playing Hardball

1. Jim Rutenberg, "Michael J. Fox, Parkinson's and Stem Cells," *New York Times*, October 25, 2006, https://www.nytimes.com /2006/10/25/us/politics/25adbox.html.

2. Steven Ertelt, "Patricia Heaton, Sports Stars Rebut Michael J. Fox on Missouri Stem Cell Ad," LifeNews.com, October 25, 2006, https://www.lifenews.com/2006/10/25/bio-1820/.

3. Rutenberg, "Michael J. Fox."

4. Ertelt, "Patricia Heaton."

5. Jesse Green, "Not Everybody Loves Patricia," *New York Times*, December 31, 2006, https://www.nytimes.com/2006/12/31/the ater/not-everybody-loves-patricia.html.

6. Stephanie Simon, "Stem Cell Dissent Roils States," *Los Angeles Times*, August 1, 2007, https://www.latimes.com/archives/la-xpm -2007-aug-01-na-stemcell1-story.html.

7. 110 Cong. Rec. S4349 (daily ed. April 11, 2007), https://congress
.gov/crec/2007/04/11/CREC-2007-04-11.pdf.

8. "Scientific Integrity and Innovation: Remarks at the Carnegie
Institution for Science by Sen. Hillary Clinton," Hillary Clinton
for President, SpaceRef, October 4, 2007, http://www.spaceref
.com/news/viewpr.html?pid=23714.

9. Steven Edwards, "McCain Stands Alone on Stem Cells," Wired,
May 4, 2007, https://www.wired.com/2007/05/mccain-stands-a/.

10. "NBC 'Meet the Press' Transcript," Vote Smart, Dec. 16, 2007,
https://votesmart.org/public-statement/310679/nbc-meet-the
-press-transcript#.XPWI1y2ZOhc.

11. Gina Kolata, "Man Who Helped Start Stem Cell War May End
It," New York Times, November 22, 2007, https://www.nytimes
.com/2007/11/22/science/22stem.html.

12. Timothy Goeglein, The Man in the Middle: An Inside Account of
Faith and Politics in the George W. Bush Era (Nashville: B&H,
2011), 57.

13. "Remarks of the President—as Prepared for Delivery—Signing
of Stem Cell Executive Order and Scientific Integrity Memoran-
dum," The White House, March 9, 2009, https://obamawhite
house.archives.gov/the-press-office/remarks-president-prepared
-delivery-signing-stem-cell-executive-order-and-scientifi.

14. Steven Ertelt, "Snowflake Babies, Pro-Life Congressmen Upset
by Obama's Stem Cell Decision," LifeNews.com, March 9, 2009,
https://www.lifenews.com/2009/03/09/bio-2783/.

15. Kolata, "Man Who Helped Start Stem Cell War May End It."

16. Dana Goldstein, "Facts About 'Snowflake Babies,'" American
Prospect, March 9, 2009, https://prospect.org/article/facts-about
-snowflake-babies.

17. Steve Chapman, "Stem-Cell Debate Myths," Chicago Tribune, June
5, 2005, https://www.chicagotribune.com/news/ct-xpm-2005-06
-05-0506050386-story.html.

18. Nicholas Wade, "Rethink Stem Cells? Science Already Has," *New York Times*, March 9, 2009, https://www.nytimes.com/2009/03/10/science/10lab.html.

19. Cheryl Wetzstein, "Obama Defunds 'Snowflake Babies,'" *Washington Times*, March 4, 2012, https://www.washingtontimes.com/news/2012/mar/4/obama-defunds-snowflake-babies/.

20. Craig Young, "Funding Cut Threatens Loveland-Based Program That Encouraged Adoption of Frozen Embryos; Women Tell Adoption Stories," *Loveland Reporter-Herald*, March 10, 2012, https://www.reporterherald.com/2012/03/10/funding-cut-threatens-loveland-based-program-that-encourages-adoption-of-frozen-embryos-women-tell-adoption-stories/.

21. Lyle Denniston, "Stem Cell Dispute Near End?," *SCOTUSblog*, January 7, 2013, https://www.scotusblog.com/2013/01/stem-cell-dispute-near-end/.

22. Erin Gloria Ryan, "Embryo Adoption: This Is Really a Thing That Is Happening," Jezebel, September 14, 2012, https://jezebel.com/embryo-adoption-this-is-really-a-thing-that-is-happeni-59 43311?tag=roe-v-world.

Chapter 13: Vindication

1. Charles Krauthammer, "Life in the Balance," *Washington Post*, June 29, 2001, https://www.washingtonpost.com/archive/opinions/2001/06/29/life-in-the-balance/af8a3e7e-75ee-457a-a91f-b357cc3e7238/.

2. Charles Krauthammer, "Stem Cell Vindication," *Washington Post*, November 30, 2007, accessed through "Technology Vindicates Morality," Townhall, https://townhall.com/columnists/charleskrauthammer/2007/11/30/technology-vindicates-morality-n89 5732.

3. Catholic News Agency, "Oprah's Website Buries Dr. Oz's 'Stem Cell Debate Is Dead' Statement," April 8, 2009, https://www

.catholicnewsagency.com/news/oprahs_website_buries_dr._ozs
_stem_cell_debate_is_dead_statement.

4. Catholic News Agency, "Oprah's Website."

5. Mollie Hemingway, "Distinctions with a Difference," Get-Religion, April 22, 2009, https://www.getreligion.org/getreligion
/2009/04/distinctions-with-a-difference.

6. Russell Goldman, "Michael J. Fox Looks Past Stem Cells in Search for Parkinson's Cure," ABC News, May 19, 2012, https://abcnews.go.com/blogs/health/2012/05/18/michael-j-fox-looks-past-stem-cells-in-search-for-parkinsons-cure.

7. Erin Allday and Joaquin Palomino, "Lofty Promises, Limited Results," *San Francisco Chronicle*, September 6, 2018, https://projects.sfchronicle.com/2018/stem-cells/politics/.

8. Wesley Smith, "California Stem-Cell Agency Wants More Voter Money," *National Review*, July 7, 2018, https://www.nationalreview.com/corner/california-stem-cell-agency-wants-more-voter-money/.

9. David Gorn, "Will State Voters Continue to Pour Money into Stem Cell Research?," NPR, January 25, 2018, https://www.npr.org/sections/health-shots/2018/01/25/579727683/will-state-voters-continue-to-pour-money-into-stem-cell-research.

Chapter 14: God's Gifts

1. Sara McGinnis, "Meet the Baby Girl Who Spent over 17 Years as a Frozen Embryo," BabyCenter, https://www.babycenter.com/609_meet-the-baby-girl-who-spent-over-17-years-as-a-frozen-embry_20001868.bc.

2. 108 Cong. Rec. H7332 (daily ed. September 22, 2004), https://www.govinfo.gov/content/pkg/CREC-2004-09-22/pdf/CREC-2004-09-22.pdf.

3. Anne Morse, "Meeting 'Leftovers,'" *National Review*, May 25, 2005, https://www.nationalreview.com/2005/05/meeting-leftovers-anne-morse/.

Epilogue

1. Steve Jobs, commencement address, Stanford University, June 12, 2005, Stanford, CA, transcript, https://news.stanford.edu/2005 /06/14/jobs-061505/.

2. Wikipedia, s.v. "Snowflake children," last modified September 30, 2019, https://en.wikipedia.org/wiki/Snowflake_children.

3. Emily Giffin, *Baby Proof* (New York: St. Martin's Press, 2006), 249.

4. Michael Rea, *Snowflakes* (Scotts Valley, CA: CreateSpace, 2016), 3.

5. George W. Bush, *Decision Points* (New York: Crown, 2010), 115.

6. Greg Laurie, "No Coincidence, Just Providence," WND, March 14, 2014, https://www.wnd.com/2014/03/no-coincidence-just -providence.

7. "Tim Tebow's Shocking Story About John 3:16 'Coincidence' Goes Viral," CBN News, January 7, 2018, https://www1.cbn.com /cbnnews/entertainment/2018/january/tim-tebow-rsquo-s-nbsp -shocking-story-about-john-3-16-lsquo-coincidence-rsquo-goes -viral.

8. From the author's transcription of the recorded broadcast, supplied to the author on CD by Focus on the Family. The show was aired August 4, 2005, by Focus on the Family Broadcast.

About the Author

JOHN STREGE IS the author of seven books, two of them *New York Times* best sellers—*Tiger: A Biography of Tiger Woods* and *18 Holes with Bing: Golf, Life, and Lessons from Dad*, coauthored with Bing Crosby's son, Nathaniel. Another book, *When War Played Through: Golf During World War II*, won the United States Golf Association's Herbert Warren Wind Book Award in 2005. John has worked for *Golf Digest* for more than twenty-two years. He and his wife, Marlene, live in San Diego County with their daughter, Hannah, the first adopted frozen embryo.